Clear & Lively
Writing

Clear & Lively Writing

Priscilla L. Vail

WALKER and COMPANY
New York

First published in the United States of America in 1981 by Walker Publishing Company, Inc.; first paperback edition published in 1994.

Published simultaneously in Canada by John Wiley & Sons Canada, Limited, Markham, Ontario

The Library of Congress cataloged the hardcover edition of this book as follows:
Vail, Priscilla L.
    Clear & lively writing.
    1. English language—Study and teaching.
2. Word games. I. Title. II. Title: Clear and lively writing.
PE1066.V34   1981   808'.042   80-54818
ISBN 0-8027-0682-7   AACR2
ISBN 0-8027-7436-9 (paper)

BOOK DESIGN: RFS GRAPHIC DESIGN, INC.

Printed in the United States of America

10   9   8   7   6   5   4   3

to
Donald Vail
lawyer, love, and linguist

Contents

Part III. Proficiency

Acknowledgments

In reckoning the professional and personal help I have received in writing this book, I am grateful and awed.

To the students who have been my teachers, to the teachers who have shared their ideas, to the teachers who have experimented with my ideas, and to their students who have slogged through the bad ones, to the researchers in the field of language development, and to the teachers and lecturers who make their findings public, thank you, through me, from the students who will benefit.

Particular thanks to:

Charlotte Goodhue, magical, magnetic first-grade teacher, whose students have produced many of the samples in this book. Being a true friend, she will try most of my suggestions once and tell me when not to try them twice.

Waldo Jones, head of the lower school at the Rippowam-Cisqua School, Bedford, New York, accurately described as having
> reverence for the power of the mind,
> knowledge of the ways of childhood, and
> acceptance of the needs of the heart.

Katrina de Hirsch, Jeannette Jansky, Sr. Winifred Danwitz, and Aylett R. Cox of the Orton Society whose wisdom, words, and ways are a model and inspiration.

Blair McElroy, editor of Independent School, skillful in her work, and generous with permissions, she lightens my load with her literate lunacy.

The National Association of Independent Schools, which, through example, publications, and conferences, champions the causes of originality, expression, and choice.

The Orton Society, which brings physicians, researchers, educators and parents together in the study of language acquisition, development, and disability. Through conferences and publications it makes sophisticated knowledge accessible to the general public. Great is its service to humanity.

Particular thanks to the students at Rippowam-Cisqua who wrote many of the examples given in this book. As burgeoning poets, novelists, and as avid game players, they bring joy to all of us who teach them.

I am grateful to the friends and family, both immediate and extended, who gave me time and privacy when I wanted them, support and criticism when I needed them, and welcome when this task was finished.

To Donald, Melissa, Polly, Lucia, and Angus, exemplars in order of appearance, thank you.

To Margaret Mayo-Smith, Omniscient ombudsperson, thank you.

To Anne and John Zinsser, keepers of quality, thank you.

To the serenity of Stonington, thank you.

To those in an older generation who are no longer here, thank you for trying to teach me when I still wasn't ready to learn.

To those in a younger generation, thank you for listening.

There are those rare people who know that something worthwhile may be inside an unprepossessing cover. As the pearl-gatherer opens the oyster, as the stew-maker peels the onions, as the gourmet plucks the artichoke, the skillful editor detects a book in the center of a first draft. Thank you, Richard K. Winslow, for enduring barnacles, onion tears, outer leaves, and choke, and for guiding me to the heart of the matter.

P.L.V.

Introduction: The Problem

This book suggests ways to write easily, clearly, and enthusiastically, a craft everyone can enjoy. The approach, a fusion of research in theories of language development and practical classroom experience, is compatible with common sense, relatively painless, and very inexpensive. Because it works, it should be accessible to everyone who cares.

Educators, citizens, and students themselves are demanding better writing skills. Our cultural expectation of instant remedies, however, encourages the development and marketing of curriculum materials which may have a temporary cosmetic effect but will not produce good writing. Like offering complexion cream to a patient with measles, too many aim at the symptoms rather than the causes.

This book emphasizes a simple truth. Many of the people who cannot write well suffer primarily from lack of exposure to good language and do not understand the reciprocity of receptive and expressive language. They need to be shown how to flip the language coin back and forth from one side to the other.

Through receptive language, the young child learns to understand the words and sentences he hears. The strength or weakness of each person's receptive language is determined first by the existence of a capacity for understanding incoming language and second by the amount and variety of the exposure he* receives through listening and reading.

Expressive language, speaking and writing, has its roots in the ground of receptive language and thrives or dies depending on the quality of the soil from which it grows.

The organization of this book reflects the relationship between incoming and outgoing language; the text describes it in detail. This introduction considers the disappointing quality of much of the written work produced today, and speculates on some possible causes. The rest of the book is divided into three more parts.

---

*Since I teach more boys than girls, the pronoun "he" comes to my mind and my pencil when I think about education. I will use it throughout the book to spare the reader an endless series of "he or she," "s/he," or "they." This choice is a reflection of custom, not bias.

Part I, The Prescription, discusses receptive language as the prerequisite of expression and provides games and activities for listening, reading, and expanding vocabulary.

Part II, Practice, discusses the various levels of expressive language proficiency in speaking and writing. It provides games and activities for developing structure, releasing imagination, and encouraging originality. One section, *Problems and Disabilities Particular to Writing*, discusses signals of specific difficulties and suggestions for help.

Part III, Proficiency, provides a twelve-month calendar of writing activities which reinforce the link between receptive and expressive activities while illustrating a variety of expressive formats.

Many of the people who lack exposure to good language also need to learn and practice the different forms of expression described throughout the book in order to avoid misinterpreting simplicity as simple-mindedness or purity of phrase as paucity of thought.

I use games, both in my teaching and in this book, because they exemplify the combination of structure and buoyancy which make up the joy of language. Many are variations on old themes, some are borrowed from other teachers, and a few are inspired originals.

At first, I thought this book would help teachers and parents of children between kindergarten and sixth grade. But in listening to educators and students I found similar language needs at many grade levels, so I widened my focus. Teachers in junior high school told me their students couldn't write. High school students, their teachers, and parents told me tales of discouragement, confusion, and poor performance. When I talked with college professors I heard bitter criticism of student work and the quality of preparation given in high school English courses.

Then I met Lydia, a young woman who teaches a compulsory course in expository writing to students at the Harvard Business School. She said, "These people don't know how to write. It's frightening. They are graduates of the best colleges and universities in the country, but they are strangers to a declarative sentence." Amazed to find ineptitude at such a high level, I repeated her remarks to an officer at a major banking house in

New York. "It doesn't stop with business schools," he said. "We require a similar writing course in our training program. Our people come out of the best business schools in the country. They are bright, ambitious, and theoretically well trained, but they seem to think they sound smarter if they use big words and lots of them. So they write gobbledegook, and what they write doesn't make sense. I got a memo the other day, and after I had read it I didn't know whether I was supposed to congratulate the guy on a triumph or fire him for incompetence!"

Still thinking the problem belonged to those under thirty, I was surprised by Daphne, a fifty-two-year-old continuing-education student. She said, "I love the idea of being back in school; I'm very interested in the subjects, but I'm terrified of writing a paper or an exam. I don't know how to write, and I don't know how to begin."

Since the relationship between listening, speaking, reading, and writing remains constant, the processes of acquiring writing skills are the same no matter what the learner's age might be. Therefore, this book is for all those who want to improve writing skills or play with different forms of written expression, either in the classroom or in less formal settings. It is for teachers or tutors in classrooms and resource rooms. It is for those who run enrichment programs for gifted and talented students. It is for those who provide extracurricular enrichment in community centers, libraries, or schools. It is for students of any age, including high school and college who would like to help themselves, either in small groups or in private. It is for parents whose children are receiving inadequate or confusing instruction. It is for families who want a pool of word games for automobile trips or dinner table enjoyment. It is for any administrator or department head who plans and coordinates the language arts curriculum. Like a cook book, it contains recipes. Like a chart or road map, it shows where to go and how to get there.

The student who develops sound writing skills stands to gain three prizes:

First, writing is a mechanism for organizing ideas and allows them permanent expression. Speaking and listening are language laid out in time. Reading and writing are language laid out in space. The former are only temporary, the latter permanent. The written word can convey the thinker's wishes, questions, insights, humor, ideas, and needs. In other words, his humanity.

Second, the person who can write his thoughts takes a huge psychological, emotional step towards autonomy and mastery as he harnesses his energy and channels his ideas through written words.

Third, the person who brings the tool of written expression to his vocation or profession has enhanced opportunities to share and lead new work in his field.

In speculating on the reasons why good writing seems rare these days, we should remember that writing, the last of the four language skills to develop, follows listening, speaking, and reading. What we hear and read will affect, and in some cases predict, what we say and write. Today, much of the language we absorb is either junk or jargon.

Junk exists in every culture. It can either be a refreshing relief from solemnity, or an enervating miasma. We have the energetic "POW" junk of comic books, advertising, and fast food; we also have the sluggish junk of uninteresting facts and tiresome stories told in clichés and turgid prose.

In much the same the way that we snatch fast food for the body, we absorb fast food for the mind, listening and speaking in phrases or slogans while relying on gesture and inflection to fill in the chinks. Although fast food is refreshing for a change, for a treat, or as a way of keeping in touch with a fast-moving world, it is not a nutritious diet of food or of language, and those who absorb only phrases will neither speak nor write complete sentences.

Soggy, glutinous junk is never refreshing. The child who absorbs the trite, the confusing, and the poorly constructed will reflect those images in writing as this eighth grader did, to her own disappointment and the displeasure of her teacher. Attempting to describe the dilemma of a love triangle, she wrote: "He asked Jane and myself to a dance and then he says 'I can't choose'. Well, like it was a bad scene."

Rubbery construction is neither entertaining nor instructive. "Multiplication tables are becoming more reliable," Fred's teacher wrote. How? Although they may be difficult to memorize, multiplication tables are known for their reliability. May Fred improve his rote work and his teacher her precision.

Jargon, also known as "semantic spinach", "psychobabble", "bafflegab" or "corporatese", turns a straight declarative sentence (I gave the car to the man in the parking lot.) into a string of multisyllabic euphemisms (The automotive device was placed under the surveillance of the vehicle placement supervisor.) Would that educators were free from such blight. George had a reading problem which persisted into third grade. His teacher, Gladys, wrote: "Development in lag structure as applied to audio-visual concepts is hoped for as a priority goal of task-orientation on the part of this boy." Good luck with your lag, George, and Gladys, "have a nice day."

If we want our children and students to speak intelligibly and to write clearly, we (parents teachers, executives, and diamond merchants, among others) must stop clogging the nation's arteries with verbal cholesterol. As I write this today our daughter and her fiancé are shopping in New York. I hope she does not, as one brochure recently urged, "develop enjewelment". Instead, I hope Norman buys her a ring because he loves her. Clear expression has value and sparkle. We must avoid the fallacy of equating simplicity and weakness. There is Brancusian beauty in a straight declarative sentence.

Two antidotes to jargon are awareness and humor. If we learn first to recognize jargon and second to laugh at it, we may develop an immunity. Pomposity invites mockery. Evelyn Waugh caused a national sensation when he stripped away the pretentiousness of funeral directors in *The Loved One*. And in the early television series "The Honeymooners," Art Carney was tuned into countless living rooms as Norton, the sewer worker, who sat around in a sleeveless undershirt proclaiming himself a "sanitary engineer." Let us consign inflated language to the humorists who make it ludicrous.

Junk and jargon foster an insidious habit which I believe crept up on us in the twenty five years between 1950 and 1975. We have gradually replaced the genuine exchange of communication with a series of one-way messages designed more to expound than exchange ideas. Many of these messages are standardized and consequently dilute the strength of spoken and written language. To my eye, we fell into the habit this way.

First, television seduced an audience away from the two-way exchange of active conversation to the one-way communication of passive absorption. Family dinner, which had previously centered around a topic, gave way to a family dinner clustered around "the tube." The absence of the give and take of verbal exchange created a vacuum which was quickly filled by sameness, slogans, and the easy-to-predict wise-cracks of "sit-coms." Captivated by an intriguing new toy, we let down our linguistic guard, allowing conversation in living rooms all over the country to be kidnapped by canned laughter.

Second came a proliferation of inflated words. People who wanted to appear important or powerful spurned short words and added syllables, choosing to *utilize* instead of *use*. It was as though they thought the power of a word could be measured by its length, or as though the recipient would be less apt to talk back to long words than short ones. In addition, internal strife over domestic politics and military involvement in foreign territory spawned a language designed to conceal rather than reveal. Its purpose was to dispense directives and statements rather than to invite comment or criticism. Such euphemistic words and phrases as *defoliation* and *megadeaths per kiloton* hoodwinked some but angered others.

The response to bloated, ambiguous language was a chain reaction of more and more one-way messages which influence the speaking and writing surrounding us today. In the 1960s the one-way messages urged: "be an individual", "tell it like it is", "let it all hang out", and "do your own thing". But we were so busy mouthing our slogans we forgot to listen to their meaning, and when the phrase "generation gap" entered our lives, we rushed to close it in our haste to be united.

Having learned from orthodontists and fashion magazines that gaps mean trouble, we forgot that they also keep things from colliding with one another. From words in sentences to mountains in ranges, gaps mark differences and preserve identities. In a search for honesty and openness that traversed economic, social and chronological lines, many people sought safety in conformity of expression and sensed danger in variety. Grammatical precision was considered fussy, and polished speech was misinterpreted as elitism. In trying for the common touch in language, large segments of our society got stuck on verbal flypaper.

Third, in a climate of "new honesty" in which "reticent" meant "up-tight" and it was prudish to value privacy, we were treated to a parade of self-disclosure whose banners offered photographs of Lyndon Johnson's abdominal scar and ever-more promiscuous details of personal lives. Self-revelation, however, is all too often merely a form of self-indulgence. Uninhibited disclosure is neither conversation nor good writing, it is catharsis or exhibitionism. Thus it adds to the supply of one-way messages already floating around in the air.

Many of us have never learned, or returned to, the exchange of real communication. This is particularly damaging to writing because the habit of receiving, sending and anticipating one-way messages saps the writer's power. The student who is accustomed to having television provide his images for him will have trouble writing vivid description. The author who inflates his prose with added syllables will entice few readers. The student whose feelings are expressed in familiar clichés will have trouble arousing his reader's emotions. And the writer who is drawn to self-disclosure as Narcissus was drawn to his own image fails to create a partnership with his reader and loses his audience.

The habit of the one-way message affects us all, but having recognized it we can try to break it, reaching out for genuine exchange of ideas, learning to receive them through listening and reading as well as to express them through speaking and writing.

While we must recognize how powerfully a writer is influenced by the language around him, as teachers we must realize that the story does not end there. In my experiences with students, my conversations with other educators, and my own struggle to be a writer, I have met six tasks which are seldom given sufficient instruction in courses or books on writing. The activities and games in this book are designed to help the writer succeed at each one.

In my experience, the writer must:
1. create partnership with his reader
2. be willing to work in isolation
3. draw the fangs from panic

4. vault or circumvent mechanical inadequacy
5. tame fear of exposure
6. overcome the influence of magic by discovering the sources of its spell

Consider these tasks one by one.

1. PARTNERSHIP

The invisible partner is an elusive creature who slips away the minute the writer forgets him. To understand the importance of this shadowy participant, consider the various functions of oral speech, inner speech, and written speech as described by the Russian Linguist Lev Vygotsky.* He shows us that the child first develops oral speech with which he labels the objects in his world and uses language to sort and interpret his experiences. Gradually these labels and constructions become soaked with personal connotations and the child moves to what Vygotsky calls inner speech.

Inner speech shortcuts the necessity for spoken words, allowing the child to move from association to association and context to context without cumbersome verbalization. Someone close to the child may share the same connotations and be able to follow his time-savers. Constant companions develop a kind of instant comprehension of idiom, but a writer who tries similar shortcuts will lose a reader who is unfamiliar with his private associations.

The writer must give a sufficiently detailed description of the scene in his head to avoid writing such sentences as, "They went there because he thought she should, and it was O.K." The ability to be a skillful escort requires a high degree of abstraction. The author's ability to sort out what he himself sees from what the reader can see depends on the writer's ability to pretend he is the reader. Pretending is the abstract skill which builds the link between the writer and his unseen companion.

The difficulties involved in developing and maintaining this kind of sense of audience are often unacknowledged in the early

*Thought and Language. Cambridge: M.I.T. Press, 1962

teaching of writing. Instead, the student is beseiged by rules of grammar, identification of parts of speech, rules for parsing prose, and counting meter in poetry. Forced to focus on mechanical terminology, he loses track of partnership and his reader abandons him.

Later sections of this book describe specific games and activities for developing and maintaining partnership and a sense of audience.

2. ISOLATION

While solitude is necessary for writing, it is anathema to a sociable student or a student at a sociable time of his life. Few children are initially tempted by something which demands seclusion and practice, a word which conjures up images of a housebound little boy perfecting piano scales while his friends play baseball outside the window. But look further.

Practicing is strange. You can't practice something until you already know how to do it. Once you know how to do it, even a little bit, you can practice and hone your performance, but until you've had one or two successes there's nothing to practice. This is true of riding a two-wheeler, playing tennis, or mastering needlepoint. After a few successes—turning the corner on that bike, a low hard shot over the net, a well-embroidered Smyrna Cross—practice is seductive. The world is filled with backboards, basketball nets, and smooth sidewalks being used by children engrossed in solitary practice. Writing can be the same if we remember what it takes to entice students into practice in the first place: success and therefore enjoyment. Part II, *Practice*, offers scores of specific games and activities and all kinds of warm-ups for all levels of writers.

3. PANIC

A thoroughbred horse, a grown man, and a student may have this in common: a plain piece of white paper produces panic. The racehorse shies or bolts, the grown man calls his secretary or makes a telephone call instead, but the student is stuck. Not being sure where to begin, what to say, or how to say it he'll probably make a few false starts, crumple them up, practice a few basketball shots to the wastebasket, develop sudden desperate needs for drinks of water and trips to the bathroom, all the while praying for some benevolent genie to blow up the school or complete the task for him. In the end, he'll either sidestep the requirement and accept a zero or put down as few words as he can get away with and move on to a less unpleasant endeavor. In other situations this student may be verbal, gregarious, and capable, but not when it comes to writing. Take George.

George is a seventh-grader who loves to talk and argue. He enjoys the language of plays, stories, and jokes, yet his English grade has never risen above a C because of his creative writing, which is invariably graded "C—too brief." His godfather, who had had similar difficulties in his own youth, taught him this trick. He said, "When you know a writing assignment is coming, fix yourself up ahead of time. Choose something you like to do and then do it, talking yourself through the experience as you go along. It doesn't matter whether it's building a model, skiing a trail, or going to the movies and buying popcorn. Putting the physical sequences and sensations into words as you carry them out will give you a huge supply of things to say when you move to paper. You won't have to hunt for words because you will have chosen them already, and you won't have to agonize over how or where to begin; you can just begin at the beginning."

George's English grade has moved up to a B. This puts him on the Honor Roll and entitles him to a free period a week which he uses for basketball practice. The system has worked so well that he has decided to expand his inventory of words and phrases by keeping a diary. A concrete approach helped George develop a new skill, and his success has enticed him into an ideal kind of practice. Practice replaced panic.

Many of the games and activities in subsequent sections are designed to banish panic once and for all.

4. MECHANICAL INADEQUACY

Difficulty with handwriting or spelling limits the writer's output. There is always a certain distance between the flow of ideas and the rate at which the writer can commit them to paper, but a wide discrepancy creates fatigue, embarrassment, annoyance, or gibberish. As teachers and guides we should remember that some students have trouble synchronizing mechanics and imagination.

Jud's hand tires easily from the cramped way he taught himself to hold his pencil. Brent's letters are crowded and indistinct from one another, making it difficult for him to reread his own words and nearly impossible for a reader to understand what he has written. Third-grader Cassie agonzies over spelling. When she intended to write "The queen was angry at the princess," she spent so much time and energy remembering *qu* and trying to spell *queen* that she omitted two key words and wrote "the queen was the princess."

The student who is a poor speller fears shame and ridicule. Polly was afraid of written work until her junior year in college when she finally bowed to inevitability and hired a friend to proofread her spelling. Her ideas were good, she always spoke up in class, and she had an excellent grasp of what was going on. An alert appearance and thoughtful statements combined to create a correct impression of intelligence which was undercut by spelling errors she could not spot in her own work. For example, writing home of dormitory life she said, "The peeple are nise, but the food is descusting!" Her papers were returned to her spattered and carved with red correction marks. She dubbed them "the bleeding beasts". When she signed up a proofreader to repair her mechanical errors, her professors could pay undisturbed attention to her ideas and her grades soared.

Chapter 6, *Problems Particular to Writing*, offers a detailed analysis of mechanical problems and suggests ways to help the afflicted student.

5. FEAR OF EXPOSURE

Writing is risky. When words are on paper and the paper is released from the hand, the writer has nowhere to hide. Fantasy, feelings, and error are there for the world to see. Most first and second graders aren't afraid; they enjoy writing stories. They tackle strong themes and avoid ambiguity: "The man saw the bear. The bear ate the man and killed him. Dead. The End." But some other students, who have struggled to tame ferocious fantasies, dare not risk putting dangerous thoughts on paper. The written word has an air of reality, and some children are afraid to risk having their powerful dreams, pleasant or unpleasant, come true. Such children will write stories that begin, I like my teacher because . . . "

Anonymity and group poetry can be safe outlets for constricted feelings. Not long ago, I was using Kenneth Koch's *Wishes, Lies and Dreams* with some preadolescent girls. Mathilda, whose mother was always picking invisible flecks of dust off her daughter's navy blue sweater, was a tightly controlled, obedient little girl. She told me solemnly that she wouldn't be able to participate in a collective poem of lies I was going to help the group compose because "lies aren't nice." I reassured her that these lies were permissable. I lied. I told her I had gotten permission from the principal. I also told her that the lies were going to be written anonymously on pre-cut slips of paper and hidden in an envelope. That way no one would know whose lie was whose. She was enormously relieved and flung herself into forbidden territory. She wrote, "I am a naughty, mean ghost. I can fly all over the world and zap everybody. Then there will only be me, and I can have everything."

Similarly, a student who is socially inept but verbally gifted may be afraid to let others know his feelings, fearing that his writing, precious to him, will be ridiculed. Steve was a fourteen-year-old closet poet. Sensitive, articulate and embarrassed by emotions, he swaggered through eighth grade, calling attention to his negative attitude and defying the rules. A perceptive teacher followed a hint Steve dropped. "You write poetry?" "Yeah." "Have you ever shown your poetry to any of your teachers?" "Nope." "Would you let me read some of it?" "O.K. I guess so." It was good. Steve had gotten tangled up in thinking that boys were supposed to be tough and rude and that expression of feelings was equivalent to admission of weakness. Freed from the net by the help of his teacher, he made peace with himself . . . and went on to win the school's English prize.

The student who is bluffing to camouflage pockets of ignorance and the student who hasn't established a point of view will fear writing and avoid clarity. A law student, caught unprepared, writes, "It might be argued that . . ." Teachers reading papers and bosses reading memos are familiar with "from time to time", "there are those who", and "one might". The user vainly hopes to imply wide knowledge.

Exposure through writing is terrifying to most people at some times in their lives and to some people at all times. Although there is no way to write without some kind of exposure, certain topics are less threatening than others, and it is our job as teachers to find and offer them. After all, not everyone wants to play Lady Godiva. The variety of expressive language activities throughout the book should help overcome this fear.

6. MAGIC

Although magic and writing skills may seem far apart, they fuse in the nature of the youthful writer or the writer who hasn't yet freed himself from youthful dependence on magic.

Magical thinking is a necessary part of a young child's social and intellectual development. It allows the child to believe that an agent, whether dressed in a top hat or Daddy's bathrobe, can make otherwise impossible things happen in a realm whose only boundaries are the limits of imagination. While he is in his period of magical thinking, it is entirely appropriate for the child to interpret all the events in his life—good and bad—as extensions of his own will. Then, like Copernicus discovering that the earth is not the center of the universe but simply part of a solar system, the maturing child sees that he is only one part of the process of life, not the cause of every event. This knowledge brings both distress and relief.

Although it is a loss to forfeit omnipotence, its departure frees the child from carrying the weight of the world on his slender shoulders. While his new realization robs him of some powers derived from magical thinking, it also confers on him the realization that he can affect his surroundings through reason and premeditated action. By discovering how the world around him works, he replaces the magic of "abracadabra" with the machinery of cause and effect.

Daily living used to nudge the child away from childish reliance on magic by providing thousands of examples of process and product. As pointed out by the late Dorothy Cohen, of the Bank Street College of Education, warming the house is a good example. In preparation for winter, fire wood would first be chopped, split, stacked, and dried. Then when the house grew cold, someone would carry in the logs, add the kindling, open the draft, light the fire, work the bellows, and reap the reward. The young child who saw the steps of preparation could anticipate the outcome.

Now, although he notices a change in temperature, he may or may not see someone move a pointer on the thermostat. If he does see the action he probably won't connect it with warmth unless someone points out the link. While we, as adults, understand why the house gets warm, we often forget to describe the hidden machinery to our children who grow up confusing automation with magic.

I made the same mistake when I took our four year old son to a large city hospital for a medical test. Being chronophobic I arrived an hour early but was too embarrassed to go into the Doctor's waiting room so much ahead of time. To protect my pride, we sat on a bench across from a bank of elevators, chatting and making short work of a box of animal crackers. When the time seemed right I suggested that we get in the elevator. He refused. I tried again. "Not going." I pleaded. "No!" Finally came the reason. "Everybody that goes in there comes out different!" Watching the automatic doors open, he had seen people go in, then the doors would close. After a while the doors would open again and PRESTO! Different people! Having spent a good part of his life in the kitchen with me, watching ingredients go into ovens and emerge transformed, he was protecting himself from a similar fate and taking no chances on metamorphosis.

Automation is so pervasive in our society and the machinery behind it so concealed that, instead of helping children outgrow reliance on magic, we are saturating them in it. Many children today depend on magic long after they should have put it in its appropriate place. This affects the student's ability to write in two ways.

First, in order to tell a story, a writer must generate his own visual imagery and take care to guide his invisible partner through it. But today's children, accustomed to having visual imagery magically provided for them every time they turn on the television set, have scant practice in generating their own. Even when they do, there is another problem.

The child who is reliant on magic himself expects instant comprehension on the part of his listener or reader, and the child who is still lodged in magical thinking does not distinguish between the imagery he imagines and what might be seen by someone who is outside his own head. It is all one and the same to him. Consequently, he cannot provide his companion with a reliable map of their common journey and is apt to leave him stranded, disoriented in a boundaryless never-never land.

Second, magic promotes passivity and instant gratification. Writing requires active involvement, but magic requires no effort on the part of the recipient, observer, or producer other than the touch of a wand, murmur of a spell, or press of a button. Magic says: "Wait and watch. Things will materialize, and what you want will appear, fully formed, of its own accord. The supermarket door will open at your approach and the shelves inside will be stocked with neatly wrapped loaves of fresh bread and vacuum-sealed jars of tangy jelly. No messy wheat sheaves. No grape vines to water." Four-year-old Taylor, defining his favorite food said, "Hamburger is a plant that grows in styrofoam boxes."

If magic is the professor of passivity, our children have learned his lesson well. Katrina de Hirsch, diagnostician of child development, wrote for the Orton Society in 1976, "Our children have not moved from the pleasure principle to the reality principle, and they retain the infantile expectation that life should provide rewards without corresponding effort."

Writing does not appear of its own accord. Like the bread and jelly in the supermarket, it is the preparation behind the scenes which produces a delectable product. The writer must exercise conscious effort using the machinery of cause and effect, the antithesis of magical thinking.

With all these obstacles before us, why should we struggle? If poor writing is pervasive, if vigor is being leeched away by junk and jargon and the road to improvement seems guarded by

Hydras, why should we bother? Can we succeed?

Leon Eisenberg, professor of child psychiatry at the Harvard Medical School, has said:

> "Linguistic competence stands at the very center of what is crucially human in each of us. We are as we speak; we work as we read; we become human as we understand each other through language."

We will struggle because we are human; we will succeed because we have the necessary knowledge. Spoken language is evanescent, but written language gives permanent form to man's deepest desires and dreams. By understanding language ourselves and by encouraging those in our care to play with the ideas and concepts outlined in this book, we can entice them to write easily, clearly, and enthusiastically.

PART I. _____

The Prescription

1.

RECEPTIVE LANGUAGE: Listening and Reading, Prerequisites of Expression

Expressive language, what we say and write, grows from receptive language, what we hear and read, just as a plant grows from a seed. Pumpkin seeds grow into pumpkins, marigold seeds into marigolds, but without seeds there would be neither fruit nor flower. In the same way, children must receive words before they can produce them.

The gardener who grows a wide variety of vegetables and flowers has a more satisfying yield than one whose crop is limited to string beans and zinnias. Plants of many different sizes, shapes, and colors can satisfy both nutritional and aesthetic tastes. Similarly, the student who has words of different "species" can harvest according to his needs. Like plants, words vary. Some are strong, others weak; some are practical, others ornamental. But a lush vocabulary does not sprout spontaneously; it must be planted and tended as it grows.

Seeds grow best in ground which has been turned, cleared of rocks, and the hard clumps of earth broken into soft dirt. Hard ground, whether a whole field or a window box, produces random crops of weeds and crusty barren patches. We can no more expect nourishing vegetables or beautiful flowers from such a garden than we can expect clarity or originality of expression from a student whose receptive language capacity is uncultivated. Words are the seeds of expression; plant them generously. If a child is unacquainted with the sounds of good language, he is like unsown, unfertilized ground in need of attention from a skilled caretaker. Teachers and parents who are interested in helping students develop good expressive skills work as tillers, sowers, cultivators, and weeders.

Our first job is to assess the student's receptive capacity. This is far more than the simple ability to hear sounds. The student must hear and also interpret them. He must identify and take meaning from the individual, spoken (or sung) words that surround him daily, maintaining order while interpreting and sorting the words as they flood in to him. Later he must learn to take meaning from words he reads as well as words he hears.

We must recognize the difference between a child who is able to absorb the seeds of language and the child with a language disability who needs to be shown how to remove or circumvent the obstacles which interfere with the growth of a network of sturdy roots.

Although this is not a textbook on how to administer or interpret a formal language evaluation, here is a way for a teacher or parent to make an informal, three-step assessment of receptive language in a listener of any age. With young children, try to work with two or three at a time, choosing ones of the same age and from the same school or neighborhood. Seeing the child in his own context gives more helpful information than simply measuring his progress against textbook norms, since what is outstanding in one milieu may be average somewhere else and what is acceptable in one set of circumstances may be below standard in another.

Step One. Read a short story aloud to the children, and then ask them questions about it. Or simply engage the group in a general discussion. Observe each student's comprehension of the following nine things. (The accompanying examples are intended as illustrations, not sample questions.)

1. *Labels.* Does he understand the specific nouns you use? Almost everybody understands cat, but catacomb, catastrophe and catamaran fit a different category.
2. *Actions.* "Run, Spot, run" is pretty plain, but how about the difference in such verbs as jog, pace, and sprint?
3. *3-Part Commands.* Ask each student to do a command

exercise. Almost everybody can follow "hang up your coat, wash your hands, and sit down at the table" because it's a routine, but how about "put this book on the corner of the table, take two steps backward, and put the newspaper under the kitchen chair?" Why does this matter? The student who has difficulty remembering and executing three-part directions will have trouble understanding and remembering verbal explanations of new, unfamiliar material, taking down homework assignments, and following directions.

4. *Plurals*. The singular and plural difference between two boys and one boy is obvious, but how about mice, people, pair, everyone, no-one, and someone?

5. *Pronouns*. I and you are elementary, but how about they and their, us and our and its?

6. *Verb Tenses*. Almost everyone understands: I jump, I jumped, I will jump, but how about: while I was jumping, now that I am jumping, and I might jump?

7. *Interrogatives*. "Do you have some candy?" is a common question, but how about "Do you think I should eat some candy?" or "Why would you like me to eat the candy?" and "What do you think might happen to me if I ate too much candy?"

8. *Active and passive voices*. Li'l Abner exemplified the difference between "the boy chased the girl" and "the boy was chased by the girl." The child who does not understand passive constructions will not differentiate between an object and an agent and his comprehension will suffer accordingly.

9. *Embedded details*. We all know who got a bump in "the boy fell down the stairs" and know who needs a bandaid in "the boy the girl saw fell down the stairs." But how about "the boy the girl saw the man push fell down the stairs?" The ability to interpret such constructions is necessary for reading comprehension beyond fourth grade.

Your student's performance will indicate which, if any, of the above nine language steps give him trouble. If he cannot interpret them correctly, he will not be able to use them correctly in his own speech, and he certainly will be unable to write them. The games and activities in this section are designed to build a facility in these nine elements.

Step Two. Pay special attention to the listener's comprehension of signal words which shift meaning. Almost everyone understands: over, under, all, none, day, night, but such terms as: every other, the ninth, each, and but are frequently misunderstood. Such words as: whenever, if, except, unless, and until are landmines to the unwary. In the course of your informal evaluation keep track of the words which give your student trouble. Later, teach him their meanings, and let him practice using them. Specific word lists and activities that use signal words are in the following chapters.

Step Three. Listen to your student's own speech and contrast it with that of his peers as you ask yourself four questions:

1. If he understands the labels, descriptions, and categories you use, does he use similar ones?
2. Does his speech include the nine types of construction described in step one?
3. Are adjectives, adverbs, pronouns, and particularly verb tenses an unselfconscious part of his conversation?
4. In contrast to others his age, how is the length, rhythm, and variety of his speech? Notice whether it comes in short utterances and phrases or in whole sentences. Does he stay with a thought, elaborate on it, and follow through to a logical conclusion? Cadence and inflection indicate an easy linguistic flow. Choppy abrupt speech may indicate interruptions in thought.

Although the answers to these questions will not give national norms or grade equivalents, when they are combined with the information gathered from steps one and two they will give an overall impression and point to specific areas of strength or confusion. Helping the adult listener expand his own awareness of language components is the first step towards providing specific and appropriate teaching for the student. The games and activities which follow are designed to enhance specific elements of the student's receptive language abilities.

2.

LISTENING GAMES AND ACTIVITIES FOR:
Sprint Listening
Scatter and Scan Listening
Aesthetic Listening

Although they may seem very different, listening and writing are similar. To write, students need to generate visual images and connect them with fact, narrative, and mood. A skillful listener, too, constantly connects words he hears with his own personal imagery. Teaching a young or delayed student the techniques of good listening is an excellent way to help him increase his ability to make his own images, a skill which today seems to be withering away. As a nation of television watchers, we are in the habit of letting the screen provide our images for us.

Merely telling a student to "listen better" or to "practice listening" is not enough. If he knew how to improve he would have done so already. He needs to be shown the different types of listening and to be taught techniques appropriate to each.

I teach my students three different types of listening. The first we call *Sprint* because, like a race, it requires an enormous amount of energy and concentration for a short time. There are special techniques which the activities will explain and illustrate.

The second kind we call *Scatter and Scan*. A listener who is confronted with a volume of words must develop a filter or seive to screen out what is superfluous so he can follow a main idea. Techniques for this kind of listening are obviously different from those used in Sprint listening and the activities vary accordingly.

The third kind is *Aesthetic*. The listener is free to join what he hears to his personal idiosyncratic imagery. There are no right and wrong answers, and originality is more prized than conformity. The difference between this kind and the previous two is apparent, and the activities for the three types vary predictably.

Do not assume that because a student is friendly and interested he is also a good listener. Katrina de Hirsch has pointed out that problems with auditory processing affect more than 25% of our student population. It is easy to be fooled by a child who nods, smiles, and maintains eye contact, as I was misled by Anne. She hadn't understood the day's lesson and needed some individual attention. As I explained the mystery of vowel pronunciations to her she nodded affirmatively, never taking her eyes from my face, giving every indication of concentration and comprehension. Puffed with pride, I congratulated myself on the clarity of my explanation, having no hint of the deflation coming my way.

"Mrs. Vail, can I ask you a question?"

Feeling the joy of teaching I said, "Certainly."

Never moving her eyes from my face and maintaining her air of concentration Anne asked, "Do you have chapped lips?" Here are activities for each of the three kinds of listening. Throughout the book the entry for each activity will include:

Title
Purpose
Level of Difficulty
Number of Participants
Materials Required
Time Required
Description

Levels of difficulty will be coded as follows:

* indicates an activity suitable for early language development, roughly kindergarten–2nd grade
** indicates an activity for intermediate language work, roughly grades 3–6
*** indicates higher level language development, roughly from 6th grade on up which matches the reading level of some college students, many high school graduates and some adults in our society
* ** *** indicates activities which are adaptable to all levels by changing some of the vocabulary. Many of the activities to follow fall in this category. Where the

principle is appropriate for all ages its application can be altered to match the students' developmental levels.

SPRINT LISTENING

Sprint listening requires focused concentration. It is necessary for remembering directions (take a left at the first light), instructions, and details. If you are told that the red headed girl in the blue dress will give you a cupcake, don't take your plate to the girl with yellow hair in the red dress or you'll go hungry.

Here follow eight Sprint activities which work well for children roughly between the ages of six and twelve. By changing the specifics to match a higher level of sophistication, the same formats can be used by students who have traded in their Teddy Bears for motorcycles. As a preliminary, teach your students three ways they can help themselves remember what they hear.

1. repeat directions aloud
2. make a mental movie. Encourage them to visualize what they are hearing
3. jot down simple notes, rebuses, pantomime, or whatever personal notation is quick and evocative

Caution: Most of the following activities are very short. Choose one and do it only once each day. The kind of concentration required is hard to sustain, particularly for those students who are having trouble. Avoid overload and build on success.

TREASURE HUNT

Purpose: following directions
Level of Difficulty: * ** ***
Number of Participants: a whole class if they are equally skillful listeners, otherwise take groups of 4 or 5 students who are on a par with one another.
Materials Required: one simple treasure
Time Required: 5 minutes per round; one round a day for two weeks will show dramatic improvement

Description: Select a simple treasure—a lollipop or candy bar works very well. One person is chosen to be the seeker and leaves the room. The treasure is put somewhere in plain sight. The seeker returns and is given precise directions of how to reach it. For instance, "Take two steps forward, three steps to the left, scratch your right ear, say your last name, look straight ahead of you at shoulder level, and you will see the treasure. Look at it, but do not reach for it until I say 'Simon says pick it up.' " If the seeker omits any steps or does any of the commands out of sequence, another member of the group can challenge him. If correct in his challenge, he usurps the role of seeker. For young children give the directions one or two at a time; for older children increase the listening load.

COMMAND ME

Purpose: following directions which incorporate prepositions, terms of measurement, and right/left discrimination

Level of Difficulty: * **

Number of Participants: 6 is an ideal number, but it can be expanded to a whole class activity if the teacher is the caller. (If you would like to play this with one student at a time, let the student race the clock by saying "How many commands can you execute accurately in one minute?")

Materials Required: for children who have right/left confusion we supply red rubber bands for their right wrists

Time Required: 5 or 10 minutes for one round

Description: Sit in a circle and choose one student to be the first commander. He gives one command or a group of commands to the player on his left. If that player carries out the command correctly, he becomes commander and gives the next instruction. For students who need practice with right/left discrimination, the commander gives such instructions as "raise your right hand", "tap your left foot", "put your right elbow on your left knee", "cross your ankles", "twiddle your thumbs", "wink your right eye", and others in which the child must identify and use left and right body parts.

Proceed to more difficult instructions such as "turn to your right", "go to the window on the left", "point to something six feet away from you", "look to the left", "name something behind you", "stand between two people", or "put your pencil underneath your shoe".

Use as many kinds of measurement as you can: "six feet away", "two feet to your left", "shoulder height", "two giant steps", "as long as your foot". Include as many metric measurements as you are comfortable with. Increase the listening load according to the expanding abilities of your students.

Use this activity, too, to practice the following 15 terms: before, after, between, beneath, first, last, middle, bigger than, smaller than, the same size as, above, below, in front, in back. Add to this list others which your students need to practice.

AIRPORT

Purpose: following directions
Level of difficulty: * ** ***
Number of participants: 6 is an ideal number, but it can be expanded to a whole class if the teacher is the caller
Materials required: a blindfold
Time required: 5 to 10 minutes per round
Description: One student is chosen to be the airplane, another student or the teacher is the control tower. The airplane student is blindfolded and given directions for landing. The control tower might say, "Take three twelve-inch steps forward, and put your left hand out to touch the desk. From the desk walk six steps forward at a 45° angle. Stop. Take one step sideways to your left. Then proceed for roughly five feet. You are on the runway. Put your hand out in front of you and walk forward until you touch a sweater for a perfect landing." As with Treasure Hunt, vary the listening load according to the capacity of

your students, and expand it to include mathematical concepts if you wish. You might say, "Go forward for the number of steps which is the total of 3 plus 2 or the difference between 7 and 9 or the denominator of 3/5 or the product of 3 times 2."

FAST

Purpose: auditory analysis
Level of Difficulty: *   **
Number of Participants: 1–10 students
Materials Required: no props needed
Time Required: 5 minutes
Description: Explain that the purpose of the game is to count the number of words in a sentence or the number of sounds in a word. Many young children don't distinguish between a syllable and a word, yet they need to isolate words from one another in order to write them, and they must understand the sequence of sounds in a word in order to spell it. Begin with counting words in sentences, using one-syllable words for starters. Here are five examples.

> The cat left.
> The cat ran home.
> The red ball is round.
> The fat pig sat in the mud.
> The bad boy stuck out his tongue.

The teacher reads a sentence aloud, the listeners count the words and hold up a corresponding number of fingers.

Next, say sentences containing compound words (mailman, snowstorm, Thanksgiving, schoolbus), names of days (Monday, today, yesterday), and familiar multisyllable words (mother, recess, vacation). When your listeners can recognize these as single words they are ready for the next step.

Ask them to count the number of sounds inside a word and to hold up the corresponding number of fingers. Begin with three-letter words (cat). Then use words with a blend at the end (last). Then add words with a blend at the beginning (plot). And finally include words with a blend at the beginning and the end (blast). There is a marked carryover from this kind of auditory analysis into later reading and spelling. The awareness the listeners develop helps them avoid skipping letters in words they read and omitting sounds in words they write.

The third step is to ask them to count the number of syllables in a word and to hold up the corresponding number of fingers. Accuracy in syllable count also carries over into reading and spelling. A reader who unlocks a long unfamiliar word syllable by syllable won't foreshorten "vaccination" to "vacation." A writer who spells one syllable at a time won't telescope "alligator" to "algator."

ALL EARS

Purpose: remembering details
Level of Difficulty: *   **   ***
Number of Participants: 1, 2 or a small group
Material Required: the teacher should have a short story or description in mind
Time Required: 5 minutes
Description: Tell the children that you are going to tell them a story filled with many details and at the end you are going to ask them to remember just one. With this kind of advance warning they won't get mad at the game—or you. Tell them to try to make a mental movie, picturing each part of the story as you say it. A sample might be, "One sunny winter day a little girl in red boots put both her mittened hands on the strap of her blue plastic sled to pull it up the hill to the house with the black shutters." Question: "What color were her boots?"

The listeners enjoy inference questions, too, if they have advance warning and don't feel tricked. An inference question for this story might be, "How do you know she wasn't eating an ice cream cone?" It is important with this, as with all other games, to start at a level which gives the players a shot at success.

STRETCH AND SHRINK

Purpose: remembering details
Level of Difficulty: *   **   ***
Number of Participants: teacher and 2–4 students
Materials required: none
Time required: 5 minutes
Description: Start *Stretch* with a very short sentence: "The boy ran." The first child repeats it. The caller then adds a detail: "The big boy ran." The second child must repeat it. Continue adding a detail as each player's turn comes. Introduce pantomime to help the children link a visual clue to an auditory stimulus. They will be delighted to discover what a help this is for remembering details. The game works best when the teacher is the caller. Just before the students are overloaded, reverse the process and play Shrink, eliminating one clause or detail until you are back at the original sentence.

Here is a story a group of fourth-grade boys successfully stretched and retold to me last December. "Last Sunday a miniature dinosaur with a bushy tail ran down the street dodging cars, bicycles, and skateboards. He ran into Carl's house looking for a hamburger, a banana, bone, or something else to eat, but all he found was Carl asleep in his pink polka-dotted pajamas." The boys were delighted at being able to remember such a long story, and one suggested counting the words. The total was impressive—forty-eight. Then Carl grinned and said, "Wait, I can make it fifty . . . The End!"

They had used the three kinds of strategies suggested in the beginning of this section:

1. repeat directions aloud
2. make a mental movie, visualizing what you hear
3. jot down simple notes, rebuses, pantomime, or whatever personal notation is quick and evocative

ZOO FOR TWO

Purpose: remembering details
Level of Difficulty: * ** ***
Number of Participants: 2 players, several pairs, or 1 caller and a whole class
Materials Required: 7 paper cups or a box with 7 compartments, roughly 70 slips of paper, and one piece of zoo paper for each participant (see illustration below)
Time Required: 30 minutes per round
Description: Set out a box with seven compartments, or use seven paper cups. Fill each container with about ten slips of paper carrying words or letters in the following categories: (1) numbers (2) colors (3) adjectives (4) body parts (5) single consonants, blends, or digraphs found at the beginnings of words (6) single vowels, vowel teams such as *oa* or *ai*, diphthongs such as *oi* or *oy* found in the middles of words and (7) consonants, blends, digraphs or letter patterns such as *tion*, *ture*, *fle*, *tle* found at the ends of words. (see sample word lists below)

If two students or groups of pairs are playing, Player A takes a piece of zoo paper which says:

MY ANIMAL
My animal has _____
_____ _____ _____
and is called a _____.
This is his picture:

Choosing one slip of paper from each cup or compartment, Player B compiles a portrait of an animal who may, for example, have *seven purple hairy ears* and be called a *groiff*. Player B reads the description to Player A, who must fill in the blanks on the zoo paper, and draw an accurate illustration. In every round each player should have one chance to listen and illustrate and one chance to compile and describe. Return the word slips to the containers for the next round, and ask the players to continue adding new words to the inventory.

If you want to play with a whole class select one student to be the caller and give the other students each a piece of zoo paper. Although the words will be the same you will find great variety in the illustrations. The role of caller can pass around by alphabetical order or by a more informal system. Be sure to keep adding new words to the containers.

After one or two rounds you may want to increase the number of categories to include such things as natural habitat or favorite food. One budding zoologist concluded his description with the information that his animal lived on top of a tin can and ate warts.

Here are some sample word lists we have used at each of three levels:

* numbers: 1–9
  colors: red, orange, yellow, green, blue, purple, white, brown, black
  adjectives: hairy, smooth, hard, soft, wet, spikey, scratchy, huge, tiny.
  body parts: limbs, head, hair, ankles, knees, ears, mouth, stomach
  initial consonants: f, k,l,m,n,r,s,t,v. We omitted b,d,p,q to avoid directional confusion, and c,g, because they have two pronunciations. Include them if you prefer.
  single vowels: a,e,i,o,u.
  final consonants: nd,st, rd,ck, ble,tle,sle,fle, listed above.

** numbers: 10–25
   colors: tan, pink, olive green, navy, pumpkin,
      gold, aqua, daffodil, lavender.
   adjectives: spongy, fuzzy, shiny, minute,
      gigantic, wobbly, stiff, extending, forked
   Body parts: limbs, head, hair, ankles, knees,
      wrists, elbows, teeth, abdomen.
   initial consonants: b,c,d,g,p,qu,bl,st,tr.
   vowels: a,e,i,o,u, oo,ee,ai,oa.
   Final consonants: nd,st, rd,ck, ble,tle,sle,fle,
      gle.

*** numbers: 3+2, 4+1, 1+3,6−1,7−5,8−6,2×2,
      3×1,3×3
   colors: mauve, violet, sandy, fuschia, royal,
      butterscotch, lime, lemon, fire-engine.
   adjectives: concave, convex, tubular,
      protruding, vertical, horizontal, bulbous,
      braided, microscopic.
   body parts: knuckles, fingernails, earlobes,
      eyebrows, molars, ribs, shins, shoulder
      blades, eyeballs.
   initial consonants: str, squ, thr, ch, sh, wh, w, y,
      gr.
   vowels: ou,ow, au,aw, oi, oy, ie, ei, or.
   final consonants: ng, rd, st, tion, ture, sion, nd,
      dge, tch.

PATTERN TRICKS

Purpose: hearing what is actually said, not what is expected
Level of Difficulty: ** ***
Number of Participants: 1 student or a whole class
Material Required: none
Time Required: 5 minutes
Description: Older students (and teachers) are usually
   confident, perhaps overconfident, of their listening
   skills. See if you can catch them in any of these four

traps. Ask them to listen to some simple questions and
give the answers as quickly and accurately as possible.

Teacher: Listen carefully. How much is 5 plus 2?
Class: 7
T: 4 plus 3?
C: 7
T: 6 plus 1?
C: 7
T: 9 minus 2?
C: 7
T: How many weeks in a day?
C: 7
T: Really?

Teacher: I am going to spell some names and words to you.
  Please pronounce them for me: M-a-c-D-o-n-a-l-d.
Class: MacDonald
T: M-a-c-T-a-v-i-s-h
C: MacTavish
T: M-a-c-N-a-i-r
C: MacNair
T: m-a-c-h-i-n-e
C: MacHine
T: Really?

Teacher: I am going to spell some words for you. Please
  pronounce them. Here's the first one: h-o-r-r-o-r-s.
Class: horrors
T: h-o-r-s-e
C: horse
T: h-o-u-s-e
C: house
T: h-o-u-r-s
C: howers
T: Really?

Teacher: I have some more spelling questions for you. What
  does this spell: p-o-t-s?
Class: pots
T: p-o-s-t
C: post
T: s-p-o-t
C: spot
T: What do you do at a green light?
C: stop
T: Really?

> Teacher: I am going to teach you a finger code for each of the five weekdays, and then we are going to use the code in a game. Here are the symbols:
>
> Monday: put your thumb sideways
> Tuesday: put your thumb up
> Wednesday: fan out all five fingers
> Thursday: cross your pointer and middle finger
> Friday: use your thumb and pointer to make a circle
>
> Fine. Now put Monday on your ear. The teacher does it with the class, and because the code is unfamiliar they watch and copy carefully.
> Class: (Obediently puts thumbs to ears.)
> Teacher: Good, now put Wednesday on your knee (demonstrates).
> C: fanned out fingers to rest on knees.
> T: Fine, now put Thursday on your elbow (demonstrates).
> C: (Confidently crosses fingers and puts them on elbows.)
> T: Good, now put Friday on your cheek (but she treacherously puts the circle on her chin).
> C: (Following her pantomime puts circles on chins.)
> T: Really: Did I say chin?
> C: groans

The point of these traps is not to make the students feel stupid but to demonstrate an important point about listening: people think they hear what they are expecting to hear. These tricks, three of which were played on an audience of 250 teachers at a conference in New York City by the Boston linguist, Eleanor Semel, are intended to be illustrative rather than remedial. A listener who has fallen into one exults in trapping his family at dinner.

SCATTER AND SCAN LISTENING

Scatter and scan listening demands an ability to sift out detail in order to find and follow a main idea. College students use this kind of listening in lecture courses, teachers use it in faculty meetings, and all of us use it in following a conversation. Teach your students to make a mental sieve which will catch necessary information and allow the superfluous to wash away. The mesh of the sieve should be woven of three kinds of organization. The first is recognition of broad categories; the next is the use of "who, what, when, where, why" to sort and analyze within categories, and the third is alertness to signal words which shift meaning. The student who has not developed a sieve for listening will probably write in a loose, disorganized way. Here are four activities.

SNAP, SNAP, CLAP, CLAP

Purpose: playing with categories
Level of Difficulty: * ** ***
Number of Participants: 6–10
Materials Required: none
Time Required: 10–15 minutes
Description: This adaptation of an old drinking song lends itself beautifully to category work. Students of all ages enjoy it. All players sit in a circle and join in a pattern of finger-snapping, hand clapping, and saying a word. One player is the starter and begins the game first by naming a category and then continuing the snap-snap-clap-clap pattern. As the turn passes clockwise, each player must volunteer a word in the selected category. For example, if 10 students were playing and the starter chose "sports", play might proceed this way:

> starter: sports
>
> all: (snap, snap, clap, clap)
> player 2: soccer
> all: (snap, snap, clap, clap)
> player 3: baseball
> all: (snap, snap, clap, clap)
> player 4: inning
> all: (snap, snap, clap, clap)
> player 5: score
> all: (snap, snap, clap, clap)
> player 6: victory

all: (snap, snap, clap, clap)
player 7: defeat
all: (snap, snap, clap, clap)
player 8: uniform
all: (snap, snap, clap, clap)
player 9: helmet
all: (snap, snap, clap, clap)
player 10: stadium
all: (snap, snap, clap, clap)

You can use sports as a broad category, as in this example, or make the game more difficult by reducing sports to subcategories: names of games (hockey, soccer), pieces of equipment (helmet, puck), indoor sports (basketball, chess). Here are eight more sample categories which may inspire you and your students to think of others.

kitchen equipment
holidays
desserts
musical instruments
leather products
entertainments
countries
things that grow

You can also combine memory practice with this game. At the end of each round, the player who speaks last must repeat all the words in order starting with his own and going back to the starter. He will probably find that looking at each player will help him remember the player's word.

CATS AND DOGS

Purpose: identification of categories
Level of Difficulty: * (for very able students) ** ***
Number of Participants: 6–10
Material Required: none

Time Required: 10–15 minutes

Description: This is a guessing game version of Snap, Snap. One person is "It" and leaves the room. When he has gone the other players sit in a circle and choose a category. "It" returns and the group takes up the pattern of Snap, Snap, Clap, Clap as in the previous game. As each player's turn comes, he says a word in the category. By listening to the words the players give, "It" must figure out what the category is, and be ready to offer a word in that category when his turn comes. He must also name the category. Here is an example. One group offered the following words as they played: eggs, flour, thermometer, margarine, recipe, oven, milk, sugar, bowl. When his turn came, "It" volunteered calories as his word to fit the category and baked goods as the overall label. If "It" is successful in deducing the category and making his contributions, he may choose the next category. The teacher may choose the next "It" or the decision may be left to the group.

WHERE OR WHEN

Purpose: recognition of the 5 wh elements and signal words

Level of difficulty: **   ***

Number of Participants: 6

Material Required: a portable radio or local newspaper

Time Required: 10 minutes

Description: Explain to your students that they are going to practice listening for the five wh elements (who, what, when, where, why). They are also going to listen for six signal words or expressions which shift meaning: *if, unless, nevertheless, but, on the other hand,* and *however* are the ones we use, but there is nothing sacred about this list. Add to it, subtract from it, or omit it from the game depending on your needs.

Assign an identity to each of your six players; one will be "who", another "what", another "when" and so forth. One player will be all the signal words. Each player is to stand up or raise his hand when he hears his element or identity. Start by telling them simple stories such as:

Last Sunday Tom and Fred decided to go out and play with Tom's new Frisbee. They went down by the river because they also liked watching the boats. However, they forgot about the river breezes. Tom sailed the Frisbee to Fred and Fred wrist-flipped it back. But when Tom tried to return it a puff of wind carried it over the water and dropped it in a passing boat.

Next, ask one of your students to bring in a portable radio. Ask him to find out what times the following news is covered on the local station: sports, local news, and world news. Begin with sports stories because it is usually easy to spot the *wh* elements in them:

The Rippowam Tigers defeated the Harvey Bears this afternoon by a score of 7–0. Rippowam Coach, Charles Goodhue, said the team had played well together; however he cautioned them against overconfidence in the return game next Tuesday. The Harvey coach was quoted as saying his team would have done better if the field had been dry and there hadn't been such a high wind.

After sports, move to local news and advertisements. The familiarity of the names of people, places, and events will help. The listeners identify the elements in such stories as this:

The Bedford Barn is having a sale on sportswear this week. All items are reduced by 25%. The store is located across from the car-wash on route 117. Beat inflation and stretch your clothing dollar. Come on in from 9–5 Monday through Saturday or 9–9 on Thursday. If comfort and style are what you like, the Bedford Barn is the place for you.

When your group has used its individual and collective sieves on familiar material, tune in to world and national news. Your students will be quick to sort such phrases as "Congress today approved . . . ", "If a price increase is not permitted, industry spokesmen warned . . . ," "Next Thursday marks the opening of . . . ", "Off the California coast today, divers found . . . "

If you prefer not to have a radio in class, read aloud from your local newspaper. Start with a sports story, move to local news, and finally to world and national events. If your group needs extra practice with such qualifiers as "on the other hand," read aloud from the editorials and letters to the editor.

The student who can organize what he hears by catching important elements in a well-constructed sieve will be alert to these same elements in material he reads. When he needs to organize his thoughts for speaking or writing the method will be familiar to him.

AESTHETIC LISTENING

Aesthetic listening demands active participation from the listener. As an accompaniment to listening, he must make his own associations and generate his own imagery, a skill which is infrequently practiced by today's students.

When a group is treated to a story unaccompanied by pictures, each listener's image of the hero, villain, and scenery is different. When pictures are provided, the imagery is standardized. Television has reduced our dependence on our own imaginations by providing ready-made illustrations.

The ability to generate crisp, original imagery is a vital skill for any writer who hopes to capture the heart and imagination of a reader. He must see clearly what is in his own mind before he can expect to intrigue others. The activities in this section are designed to give students practice in original representation.

ANTICIPATION

Purpose: anticipation of a story line
Level of Difficulty: *   **   ***
Number of Participants: any number from 1 to a whole class
Materials Required: a 5 or 10-minute story for the teacher to read aloud
Time Required: 15 minutes beyond the listening time

Description: Choose a story to read aloud. Warn your
listeners that you are going to stop just when it gets
really exciting. If you warn them ahead of time, it's fair to
do it. When the suspense mounts, stops. Then ask them
to try to predict what the writer of the story will say next.
It always amazes me how many different continuations
a group of listeners can invent.

ALTERNATE ENDINGS

Purpose: shifting a story line
Level of Difficulty: *   **   ***
Number of Participants: any number from one to a whole
class
Materials Required: a 5 or 10-minute story for the teacher to
read aloud
Time Required: 15 minutes beyond the listening time
Description: The principle is just the same as *Anticipation*,
but it differs in this way. Stop reading when the
suspense mounts or just before the ending. Ask your
students to try to anticipate the author's conclusion but
then have them invent a *different* one. Imaginative
students enjoy this, and their offerings are
unpredictable and delightful. Concrete thinkers are
uncomfortable, and they have trouble moving beyond
paraphrasing what they think the author would say.

LISTEN AND INTERPRET

Purpose: playing with imagery
Level of Difficulty: *   **   ***
Number of Participants: a small group or a whole class
Materials Required: a poem or a story for the teacher to read
aloud, a recording of music without words for the
teacher to play, and supplies for drawing, painting, or
collage

Time Required: allow anywhere from 30 minutes to 2 hours beyond the time required for hearing the selection, depending on the age and concentration span of the group.

Description: You can do this with a large or small group, and since it works equally well with music and words it is fun to alternate them. If you decide to start with music, begin by humming a few familiar tunes such as "Jingle Bells" and "Happy Birthday." Ask your students what they associate with the music and see if they can visualize an image or a scene rather than simply saying the words *Christmas* or *birthday cake*. Let them take turns humming some familiar commercials to see what mental pictures those evoke.

Then tell them you are going to play some unfamiliar music to find out what each person will see in his mind's eye. In choosing the selections, try to find a variety of instruments as well as different types of music. A brass ensemble, flute, banjo, organ, full orchestra, and synthesizer evoke very different responses.

Students of all ages are intrigued by trying to interpret animal calls. If you think your group would like to try, here are three recordings.

1. *The Language and Music of the Wolves*, Columbia C30769
2. *Deep Voices (Whales)* Capital #11598
3. Andre Kostelanetz Conducts the Music of Alan Hovhaness, Columbia M34537

The first two are animal calls with some narration. The third record contains a selection titled, "And God Created Great Whales," which interweaves whale voices with orchestral music composed in similar pattern and melody. The result is beautiful and strange.

Play your selection once or several times, and then ask your students to illustrate it. They will delight in one another's interpretations, and the results make a fine display.

If you would rather begin with a verbal selection, choose a story or poem which is unfamiliar. After you have read it ask each of your listeners to close his eyes and think about any part which was particularly appealing. Ask them each to make a descriptive drawing, painting, or collage of that part. One student may want to draw pictures of the main characters, while another may want to retell the story in a cartoon series of four or six frames. One student may want to paste together a collage which recalls one episode, and another may want to capture the essence of the whole story.

People are not all alike, and each person's imagination can produce something different. Particularly with children, the originality matters as much as the artistic merit of the finished product. Our students, exposed as they are to television, need a variety of imagery—novel and unpredictable—to avoid being sedated by visual Valium.

LOOK, LOOK, GOBBLEDYGOOK

Purpose: using nonsense for imagery and onomatopoeia
Level of Difficulty: * ** ***
Number of Participants: a small group or a whole class
Materials Required: the poems below, any other nonsense
      selections you enjoy
Time Required: flexible depending on the age of the group
      (see specifics below)
Description: We used poems by Edward Lear and Lewis
      Carroll for students at three levels. "The Owl and the
      Pussy-cat" appeals to all three age groups. Although the
      tale is ludicrous, it has an intelligible story line which
      makes it a fine introduction to nonsense work.

THE OWL AND THE PUSSY-CAT

The Owl and the Pussy-cat went to sea
    In a beautiful pea-green boat:
They took some honey, and plenty of money
    Wrapped up in a five-pound note.
The Owl looked up to the stars above,
    And sang to a small guitar,
"O lovely Pussy, O Pussy, my love,
    What a beautiful Pussy you are!"

Pussy said to the Owl, "You elegant fowl,
    How charmingly sweet you sing!
Oh! let us be married; too long we have tarried:
    But what shall we do for a ring?"
They sailed away, for a year and a day,
    To the land where the bong-tree grows;
And there in a wood a Piggy-wig stood,
    With a ring at the end of his nose.

"Dear Pig, are you willing to sell for one shilling
    Your ring?" Said the Piggy, "I will."
So they took it away, and were married next day
    By the turkey who lives on the hill.
They dined on mince and slices of quince,
    Which they ate with a runcible spoon;
And hand in hand, on the edge of the sand,
    They danced by the light of the moon.

Edward Lear

After the students heard it several times we asked them some questions. Three first graders who were asked what they thought a bong-tree would look like said:

"It's just like a palm tree."

"It makes noise. It's just one big round bong that grows up out of the ground."

"It's just like an apple tree except it grows bongs."

To my question "What are bongs?" came the reply "Mean little sour green things."

Then we asked, "What is a runcible spoon?"* Here are some answers from various ages. Look them over and collect some new ones from your students.

Kindergartener: (solemnly) My mother has one.
2nd grader: big . . . so you could put lots on it.
4th grader: one that was left there by pirates
6th grader: made of a very valuable metal
8th grader: shiny
10th grader: like a sieve, so all the juice would drain off.
12th grader: of superior design, with a fancy looped handle.

Since Lewis Carroll's "Jabberwocky" is made up almost completely of nonsense words, children find it harder to interpret than "The Owl and the Pussycat." First and second graders are either annoyed by it, or they just shrug and say, "I don't get it." Save it for fourth graders or older students who, having played with the imagery of bong-tree and runcible spoon will be eager to try a new selection.

JABBERWOCKY

'Twas brillig, and the slithy toves
   Did gyre and gimble in the wabe:
All mimsy were the borogroves,
   And the mome raths outgrabe.

"Beware the Jabberwock, my son!
   The jaws that bite, the claws that catch!
Beware the Jubjub bird, and shun
   The frumious Bandersnatch!"

*Webster's New World Dictionary defines runcible spoon thus: a table utensil of indefinite form referred to by Edward Lear in his humorous poem "The Owl and the Pussycat" (1871): later applied to any of various utensils with broad tines in a spoonlike shape.

He took his vorpal sword in hand:
    Long time the manxome foe he sought—
So rested he by the Tumtum tree,
    And stood awhile in thought.

And, as in uffish thought he stood,
    The Jabberwock, with eyes of flame,
Came whiffling through the tulgey wood,
    And burbled as it came!

One, two! One, two! And through and through
    The vorpal blade went snicker-snack!
He left it dead, and with its head
    He went galumphing back.

"And hast thou slain the Jabberwock?
    Come to my arms, my beamish boy!
O frabjous day! Callooh! Callay!"
    He chortled in his joy.

'Twas brillig, and the slithy toves
    Did gyre and gimble in the wabe:
All mimsy were the borogroves,
    And the mome raths outgrabe.
                                                            Lewis Carroll

You may wish to follow these four steps.
Step 1. The teacher reads the poem while the students simply listen and soak up the sounds.
Step 2. The teacher writes the poem on the board, reads it aloud while the class listens, then each student copies it. The children soak up the visual pattern of the nonsense words as well as the sounds.
Step 3. The teacher and class read the poem in unison, each student reading from his own copy. The children see and hear the nonsense in their own handwriting and voices.
Step 4. Give the students this written exercise:

   1. If if were brillig outside would you be glad or sorry?

2. Describe a slithy tove.
3. List three of the Jabberwock's physical characteristics and three words describing his personality.

Here is a sample response from one student:

1. I would be glad. Brillig is like snow made out of feathers. It only falls about once a year and when it happens, everyone gets a holiday.
2. Slithy toves are wet round worms. Nobody likes to touch them. Brillig sticks to them and they like the feeling.
3. The Jabberwock is powerful with a strong beak and a huge head. He is cruel, impatient, and jealous.

3.

READING GAMES
AND ACTIVITIES FOR:
Accuracy Reading
Survey Reading
Pleasure Reading

In speaking and listening, words are abstract representations of objects and ideas. Reading requires an additional level of abstraction, using a printed symbol to represent a spoken one. Some teachers feel that students should always read silently, taking meaning directly from what they see. However, experience tells me that even when reading silently it is important for students to read with their ears as well as with their eyes, hearing the rhythm of prose, the sense of a pun, and the music of poetry. The student who listens to his own silent or oral reading harnesses logic to his work and gives himself an additional check on accuracy while cutting down on such errors as:

"The dog ate his foot."
"Does that make sense?"
"No, but that's what it says."
"What does your dog eat?"
"His food—oh, I get it!"

Reading, like listening, falls into three categories: accuracy reading, survey reading, and pleasure reading. Of course, these three categories overlap, but understanding the differences helps a student improve his reading. Furthermore, familiarity with the structure of each type helps a student become a skillful writer. Here is an eloquent expression of the symbiosis between reading and writing, composed by a ten-year-old boy who was overcoming disabilities in both receptive and expressive language.

I used to be smaller than a pencil, but now I am bigger than most
   of my friends.
I used to like to pretend I was Batman, but now I really am Me.
I used to be scared of being home alone, but now I am not.
I used to wear anything I wanted to school, but now I wear a shirt
   and tie.
Last year I was 9, but this year I am 10.
Last year math was easy, but this year it is hard.
Last year I thought it was funny when a friend of mine fell in the
   swimming pool, but this year I laugh when my friend tells me a
   joke.
And the biggest difference in me is I can read.

by Josh Canning

Three basic games, Old Maid, Concentration, and Bingo
will be used with variations throughout the book. Since they are
introduced in this section, this seems a good time for overall
directions on how to make and play them.

1. OLD MAID (SOMETIMES CALLED ODD MAN OUT, JOKER, OR KISS A GORILLA)

Purpose: pairing words
Number of Participants: 2–4
How to Make and Play It: How many pairs of cards you want in
   your deck depends on the age of your students and the
   size of your word list. Anywhere from fifteen to twenty-
   five pairs is workable. Write each word on two cards,
   thereby creating pairs. Draw a picture of an old maid,
   odd man, or a gorilla on one odd card. Don't worry about
   the caliber of your art work; your students will be
   tolerant.

   The entire deck of cards is dealt out to the players.
   Each player looks among the cards in his own hand for
   pairs. When his turn comes he will read the word aloud
   and place the paired cards face-up on the table. The
   player to the left of the dealer, Player A, goes first. He
   plays any pairs he has in his hand and then picks a card
   from the player on his left, Player B. If the card he

chooses matches a card he already holds, he plays the pair. If it does not, it is then Player B's turn. He plays whatever pairs he has in his hand and picks a card from Player C. The game continues, each player picking a card from the person on his left and making pairs until one player is stuck with the odd card. He is the loser. In the case of Kiss a Gorilla, he must kiss the picture on the card.

2. CONCENTRATION
(SOMETIMES CALLED PAIRS, PAIR-UP, MEMORY, OR TWO BY TWO

Purpose: pairing words

Number of Participants: 2–4

How to Make and Play It: Like *Old Maid*, the deck of this card game uses pairs of words, one word to a card. Unlike *Old Maid*, there is no left-over card, and because all cards are spread out on the floor or a table instead of being held in a player's hand, there can be more cards in each deck. Choose any number between fourteen and fifty-two, depending on your players or word list.

The dealer deals the entire deck out, putting the cards face down on the floor or table. Rules vary as to whether they may be spread out in random fashion or must be in rows and columns. Suit yourself. The player to the left of the dealer, Player A, turns up any two cards, hoping to make a pair. If he does make a pair he keeps it and takes another turn. If he does not make it he must turn both cards back down, leaving them in their original location. All players must be able to see the cards as they are turned up. Play passes clockwise to the next person, Player B, who, trying to remember what cards Player A has turned up, turns up any two cards in search of a pair. Play continues until all the cards have been paired. The player with the most pairs wins.

3. BINGO

Purpose: word recognition

Number of Participants: 1–12 but 4 is my favorite for reasons explained below

How to Make and Play It: Draw a 9- or 25-space grid on a piece of 8 1/2" X 11" paper. I use nine-space paper for young children and twenty-five-space paper for older students. Mark the center space "free", "Bingo", or "Good Luck!"

Write the words you wish to teach on the paper in random order, one word in each space. Each player's paper must use the same words but in a different arrangement. Making up a game for twelve players requires twelve rearrangements. This is time consuming for the maker and is why I prefer playing with four at a time. The caller keeps a master list of the words for each game.

Each student has a Bingo paper and a sufficient number of tokens to put one on each of the nine or twenty-five spaces. Cut out squares of colored index card for tokens or use raisins or mini-marshmallows for a treat. Some teachers use pennies, but I prefer to keep money out of the classroom. As the teacher holds the master list and calls the words from it, one at a time, each player puts a token on a space containing the word he hears. The first player to cover all the spaces in any column, row, or diagonal line calls out *Bingo* and is the winner. If the group wants to see who comes in second, or if the players want to try for double or triple *Bingo*, keep on playing.

You can also play *Bingo* with a single student. Say, "Let's see how quickly or how slowly you get *Bingo*." Then, turning your back so you cannot see the player's card, call the words. Be sure to notice what time you start and when the player calls *Bingo*. Inform him of these times, and let him figure out how long it took.

ACCURACY READING

The Internal Revenue Service and the Bureau of Motor Vehicles both insist on precise, accurate reading. Job application forms, insurance policies, and directions on how to assemble a toy Apache fort after midnight on Christmas Eve also require it. Accuracy reading is slow, and errors bring a stiff penalty. Here are five pleasurable activities which help polish performance to a high gloss.

QUIT IT, QUICK

Purpose: accurate discrimination of words of similar
  configuration
Level of Difficulty: ** ***
Number of Participants: 2–4
Materials Required: teacher-made deck of cards
Time Required: 1–15 minutes
Description: Play it as *Old Maid* or *Concentration* using a
  deck of *qu* words
  Here is a sample word list:

  quit
  quite
  quiet
  quick
  quip
  quiz
  quilt
  quibble
  quack
  quake
  quart
  quote

The odd card can have the word *question*. Add other words if you want to make a larger deck, or have each word appear four times instead of twice, requiring the player to collect all four.

A THOROUGH THOUGHT

Purpose: accurate discrimination of words of similar
      configuration
Level of Difficulty: **   ***
Number of Participants: 2–4
Materials Required: teacher-made deck of cards
Time Required: 10–15 minutes
Description: This also lends itself to Old Maid or
      Concentration. Here is a sample word list to make
      sixteen cards:

> tough
> trough
> though
> thought
> through
> thorough
> throughout
> throat

If any of your students have more than the usual
amount of trouble with these words, make the following
color-coded master card and leave it on view
throughout the game. Write the words using 5 colors.

> Use red for *th*
> Use black for *ough*
> Use orange for *r*
> Use yellow for *o*
> Use pink for final *t*

Color emphasises the distinguishing features of these
confusingly similar words.

> **through, thorough, thought**

SAME OR DIFFERENT BINGO

Purpose: rapid discrimination of words of similar
    configuration
Level of Difficulty: *   **   ***
Number of Participants: 2–4 is ideal, but add more if
    necessary
Materials Required: 9 or 25 space Bingo paper and an
    appropriate number of tokens
Time Required: 15 minutes
Description: This *Bingo* game uses pairs of words which
    students frequently mistake for one another, such as
    "ever" and "even." If you are using nine-space game
    paper choose four pairs from the list below. If you are
    using twenty-five-space paper choose twelve pairs. Go
    over the list carefully with your students before you
    start to play, discussing the similarities and
    distinguishing features of each pair. This will help the
    players select accurately. As the caller you may wish to
    give an extra reminder by saying, "Ever (with an
    emphasis on the r), not even (with an emphasis on the
    n)." Here is a word list we use. Add to it.

went — want	of — off
place — palace	from — form
could — cold	if — it
horse — house	beard — bread
were — wear	kitchen — kitten
word — world	started — stared
father — farther	licks — likes
plant — paint	work — walk
ever — even	supper — super
lamp — land	very — every
small — smell	except — expect — exact
for — far	

CODES

Purpose: accurate sequencing of letters to sharpen precision in reading and spelling

Level of Difficulty: *   **   ***

Number of Participants: small group or a whole class

Materials Required: index cards, sample of Morse Code (see illustration)

Time Required: this can be a 30-minute exercise or a whole unit

Description: Students from first grade through graduate school enjoy cryptography. Here is the Morse Code and a way to use it in class:

MORSE CODE

A	●—	N	—●
B	—●●●	O	———
C	—●—●	P	●——●
D	—●●	Q	——●—
E	●	R	●—●
F	●●—●	S	●●●
G	——●	T	—
H	●●●●	U	●●—
I	●●	V	●●●—
J	●———	W	●——
K	—●—	X	—●●—
L	●—●●	Y	—●——
M	——	Z	——●●

Display the code where everyone can see it. Ask your students to write their names in code on index cards. Shuffle the cards and pass them around. Can the students recognize one another's names? Post the cards on a bulletin board and see if anyone can read all the names. Next, ask each student to pick a riddle and write the question in traditional letters and the answer in Morse Code. Pass the riddles around. Can everyone read the answers?

Next, ask each student to think of an interesting question of the day. Assign a day to each class member. When his day comes it is his job to write his question of the day on the blackboard in Morse Code for everyone to read and discuss.

When your students are familiar with a standard code such as Morse, encourage them to invent new codes by substituting letters of the alphabet for one another or by using numbers or symbols of their own invention to represent letters. In translating words into a code other than the alphabet, students practice and reinforce accurate sequencing of letters. This exercise has a marked carryover to reading accurately.

SLEUTHS ON THE LOOSE, FINGERPRINTING

Purpose: accurate visual discrimination of detail, categorizing

Level of Difficulty: ** ***

Number of Participants: 4 is ideal, but it could be expanded to include a whole class.

Materials Required: index cards, magnifying glass, ink pad, and description of fingerprint types (see below)

Time Required: short play — 45 minutes
long play — five 45-minute sessions

Description: Begin with a general discussion of fingerprints. Pass the magnifying glass around and ask the students to look at their own fingers, emphasizing that each person's pattern is unique. Then introduce them to the following four major categories: arches, loops, whorls, and composites or accidentals.

1. *arches*: ridges run from side to side with no backward turn

2. *loops*: some ridges make a backward turn, but do not twist

3. *whorls*: some ridges turn a complete circle

4. composite or accidental: combinations or deviations

For the short play let each student use the ink pad, an index card, and the magnifying glass to make and analyze his own print.

For the long play you might want to do what I did with four fourth grade boys. First, we studied some sample prints and learned to spot directional differences in the swirls. We found that tracing them and duplicating them with our fingers helped. Then we learned two sub-categories of loops (ulnar loops face the little finger and radial loops face the thumb), and we learned to distinguish a tented arch ($\bigwedge$) from a plain arch ($\frown$). Armed with this knowledge, the boys set out with an ink pad to record each classmate's thumbprint on an index card. They wrote the classmate's name on the left hand side of the top line and coded the right hand corner with one mark for print type and one for sex, M/F. When all the prints were taken, analyzed, and each card marked, we had perfect materials for an endless game of categorizing. We made charts analyzing the following: most common type, least common type, number and names of girls (listed alphabetically by last name) with each type, the same for boys, and then the difference in the numbers of girls and boys in each category. In races to see who could be first with the correct answer, we used such questions as, "How many people in the last half of the alphabet have ulnar loops?" We produced new, un-analyzed prints for on-the-spot scrutiny and awarded one point to the first person who could categorize each correctly.

This exercise produced a marked carryover to the mechanics of more accurate reading; the boys saw the similarity between the direction of a loop and the direction of a letter, and between the design of a print and the configuration of a word.

SURVEY READING

Survey reading is to reading what *Scatter and Scan* is to listening. The reader must cover a lot of material, identifying the main topics, sorting out minor details, and storing major ones. Like rubbing your stomach and patting your head at the same time, it takes practice and coordination. Above all, effective survey reading requires a well-constructed organizational sieve which should be made of the following four components: identification of the primary topic, understanding of the vocabulary, recognition of the five *wh* elements, and anticipation of likely outcome. Here are activities to help your children with each of the four:

FRAMEWORK

Purpose: finding the main idea
Level of Difficulty: ** ***
Number of Participants: 1 or 2 at a time, initially, then a whole class
Materials Required: a short story on the students own level
Time Required: 45 minutes
Description: By nature a child is a collector not a winnower. He learns his world by amassing experience and absorbing detail. But in order to find a main idea, he must sort out and discard any irrelevant distractions even though they may be tantalizing. In effect then, we ask him to learn in a way which is opposite to his habit. No wonder children have trouble finding the main idea. Here is a way to help.

First, let your student find the framework in familiar material before you ask him to discover one in something unfamiliar. This way the structure will be a support to him, not a trap door. Reverse the usual teaching procedure by starting with the answer. For example you might say, "This story is mainly about a boy who is poor, hungry, and lonely. He wins a $100 prize and a dog." Then summarize the rest of the story for him according to the five *wh* elements: who,what,when, where,why. Finally, read the story together. Leave plenty of time for discussion. Then, and not until then, ask him to find the sentence that tells him the story is mainly about a boy, the sentence that sets up the conflict, the sentence that keeps the reader in suspense, and the one which provides a conclusion.

With the next story give him two possible main ideas, follow the procedure outlined above, and ask him to choose which main idea fits the story best. Read a third story together, identify the five *wh* elements with him, and ask him to provide the main idea.

If your students are equally proficient, do this with the whole class. If there is a gap, work with the slower students in pairs or small groups to prevent discouragement.

STOCKPILE

Purpose: vocabulary preview
Level of Difficulty: *   **   ***
Number of Participants: pairs or small groups
Materials Required: Old Maid cards, Concentration cards, or
   Bingo paper and tokens
Time Required: 30 minutes
Description: When a student meets familiar vocabulary in a
   text, the words are like signposts. Unfamiliar words are
   stumbling blocks. If a reader has to stop and wonder
   what a word means, he loses momentum. If he skips
   over it his comprehension suffers accordingly.

   Select whatever vocabulary your students will need
from the materials you are planning to use. Give them
practice recognizing and defining the words. Use *Old
Maid, Concentration*, or *Bingo*. If you choose either of
the first two, require players to define the words as they
pair them. In *Bingo*, the caller should call each word in a
sentence as well as saying it in isolation. Here are some
starters and representative word lists.

2nd grade. *Topic: The Circus,* acrobat, parade,
   trainer, ringmaster, aerial, trapeze
   pachyderm, clown, sealion, feline.
4th grade. *Topic: Geography,* plain, mountain
   range, peak, pass, river, tributary, silt,
   soil, nutrient.
6th grade. *Topic: Weather,* cumulus, mackerel,
   cirrus, overcast, Celcius, Fahrenheit,
   frigid, humid, precipitation.
8th grade. *Topic: Mythology,* mythical, factual,
   imaginary, animism, minotaur, maze,
   Greek, Roman, Norse, revenge.
10th grade. *Topic: First Aid,* fracture, sever, pressure,
   resuscitate, clamp, shock, dilation,
   artery, obstruction, abdominal.
12th grade. *Topic: Governments,* oligarchy
   monarchy, hierarchy, democracy,
   plutocracy, aristocracy, republic,
   legislature, legal, judicial.

ELEMENTS

Purpose: recognition of the 5 *wh* elements: who, what, when, where, why

Level of Difficulty: *   **

Number of Participants: 5

Materials Required: 5 containers, each holding 10 word cards

Time Required: 30 minutes

Description: Label each of the five containers with one of the *wh* words. Put ten cards containing words of the appropriate category in each container. Here are five sample word lists:

Who	*What*
the alligator	ate a balloon
Joe	shot off a firecracker
the ballet dancer	went on a trip
the lion tamer	visited his brother
the carpenter	wrote a book
my teacher	read a poem
your uncle	sang a song
a policeman	heard a horn
my parents	drove a nail
the whole class	got a splinter

When	*Where*
today	up the chimney
yesterday	in the supermarket
tomorrow	at the movies
last week	beside the door
at midnight	over the roof
at dawn	under the chair
at three o'clock	everywhere
around supper time	in the drawer
in 1845	outside
on his birthday	indoors

Why
because it was cold
since he was late

because the dog left
because my father said to
because the room was too small
because the balloon popped
because I had the giggles
because they were chicken
since we all wanted to
since it was a surprise

Start by explaining that stories are made up of these elements. You are going to put them together in a nonsense tale. Ask each of the five players to pick a word card from one of the containers. Proceeding in order (who, what, when, where, why), each student contributes his word or phrase. A sample story from these lists might be: The alligator ate a balloon around supper time outside because the room was too small. Ask the group "*who* was in the story, *what* did he do, *when, where and why?*"

Then ask each participant to take one phrase card from each of the containers. Each player makes and writes out his own absurdity story. The stories are passed around, and the readers must be prepared to identiy the *wh* ememnts. You might combine this with an exercise in following directions by saying, "Put an orange dot on the *who*, draw a red line under the *what*, circle the *when*, cross out the *where*, and put a dotted square around the *why*."

WHO'S ON THIRD

Purpose: practice with passive construction and embedded detail
Level of Difficulty: **   ***
Number of Participants: pairs of students
Materials Required: deck of cards, each containing 2 sentences and a question (see below)
Time Required: 30 minutes

Description: This is a challenge card game for players who need to refine their recognition and understanding of passive construction, agent and object, and that backbone of gossip, who-did-what-to-whom. Take a stack of index cards and on each one write two statements and a question. The first player picks a card, reads both statements aloud, and answers the question. Each correct answer earns the player a point. Play alternates, and the highest score wins. Here are some samples:

> The fat fireman's wife went home.
> The fireman's fat wife went home.
> In which statement was the woman fat?
>
> The boy pushed the girl.
> The boy was pushed by the girl.
> In which statement was the boy the victim?
>
> The dog was chased by the cat.
> The dog was not chased by the cat.
> In which statement was the dog safer?
>
> The man saw the boy on the stairs.
> The man was seen by the boy on the stairs.
> In which statement did the boy do the looking?

WHAT'S COMING

Purpose: previewing a topic before meeting it in formal study
Level of Difficulty: ** ***
Number of Participants: whole class or small group
Time Required: 30–45 minutes
Description: This reversal of the usual *read and discuss* procedure is excellent preparation for the study of a complicated topic. Help your students brainstorm about a topic *before* asking them to study it. The process of forming ideas and opinions in advance lays an adhesive surface to which new facts and ideas can stick.

    For example, a sixth-grade teacher was planning to

explore the impact of the automobile on society. She
began by asking her class these questions:

Have there always been cars?
How did people get around before there were cars?
What influence do you think horse, foot, and bicycle
   travel would have on friendships, schooling,
   recreation, and community life?
What would be some of the advantages of the above?
What would be some of the disadvantages?
Which do you think would cost more to buy and
   maintain: a horse, a bike, or a car? Which requires
   the most equipment?

The students amassed quite a few opinions and
images of their own and were proud to discover the
power of their own reasoning. They were excited at
testing their own conclusions against those of
historians. As the study progressed, the comment that
is a teacher's bane, "I don't know . . . I forget", was
shoved aside by, "Oh! I never thought of *that*". The
reader who has learned to organize incoming
information is familiar with the tools to organize his
writing.

PLEASURE READING

Hammocks, comfortable chairs, and window seats with
quilts are ideal settings for *Pleasure Reading*, as are the suspended
time of a train, bus, or airplane trip, an unprogrammed August
afternoon or a snowbound day. Sadly, few children associate this
kind of reading with school. Yet, encouraging a child to develop
personal literary tastes and giving him time to pursue topics of
interest provides ideal exposure to language as well as emotional
and aesthetic satisfactions. The vocabulary and linguistic
rhythms a student absorbs from his pleasure reading become a
major resource for his expressive work. Since individual tastes
differ and should be honored, it is hard to standardize and codify
the next two suggestions.

READ AND SHARE

Purpose: developing aesthetic expression from receptive activity

Level of Difficulty: *   **   ***

Number of Participants: unlimited

Materials Required: reading selected by the student, paper, and simple art materials

Time Required: as much as the teacher is willing to allot, 5 15-minute sessions being less satisfying than one or two longer ones. These can be begun in school and carried over into homework.

Description: Students should be free to choose the topic and level of their own pleasure reading. It may range from animal lore to adventure stories to a motorcycle manual, as long as the reading is followed by some form of expression. For example, after reading *Uncle Tom's Cabin* a sensitive fourteen year old girl, who had hesitated to put her feelings into words, choreographed and danced the story of Liza crossing the ice for her class as an alternative kind of book report. After watching her dance three other students decided to read the book, and she herself was asked to perform the dance at the final all-school assembly.

As a variation on a standard oral or written report, a student who has read a fairy tale may want to make puppets of the characters and give a show. A student who has read a biography of Catherine the Great may want to make drawings of period costumes or a sketch of her palace. The frontier tale enthusiast may make a diorama in a shoe box, and a demonstration of a tool and repair kit might follow the reading of a motorcycle manual. Expressive activities provide an outlet for enthusiasm, give the student a chance to share a corner of himself with his classmates, and enhance the pleasure of reading.

LISTEN HERE, LISTEN HEAR

Purpose: exposing the students to the sounds of good
　　　language and literature
Level of Difficulty: * ** ***
Number of Participants: unlimited
Materials Required: a story
Time Required: 15 minutes at the end of the school day is
　　　ideal.
Description: This is nothing more complicated than choosing
　　　a story and reading it aloud to the class. Sharing a story
　　　creates a special bond among those who hear it
　　　together. Little children frequently convert the physical
　　　closeness and common focus into powerful affection
　　　for the reader, finding nourishment in the emotion itself
　　　as well as in the story. Elementary school children catch
　　　the vocabulary and cadence of textured language as
　　　surely as they catch a holiday mood. Students in junior
　　　and senior high school absorb nuances in vocabulary
　　　and enjoy identifying with characters who face
　　　emotional dilemmas similar to their own.

　　　　No one is too old to benefit from *hearing* literature.
　　　Remember that the student who has never been
　　　absorbed in a good story will be unable to write one.

　　　　I offer this list of titles with trepidation since tastes
　　　and interests vary so widely. Remember that
　　　enthusiasm and reluctance are equally contagious.
　　　Only read aloud a story you yourself enjoy.

　　Kindergarten: *Bedtime for Frances*, by Russell
　　　　　　　　　Hoban. The story pokes gentle fun at
　　　　　　　　　a fear many kindergarteners share.
　　　1st grade: *Stuart Little*, by E. B. White. Even
　　　　　　　　　children who are familiar with the plot
　　　　　　　　　enjoy hearing the story again.
　　2nd grade: *If I Ran the Zoo*, by Dr. Seuss. 2nd
　　　　　　　　　graders enjoy such giant nonsense
　　　　　　　　　words as Fizza-ma-wizza-ma-dil.
　　3rd grade: *Just So Stories*, by Rudyard Kipling.

These are a good length and the humor is on target.

4th grade: *The Bad Island*, by William Steig. The language is rumbling, humorous, and magnificent.

5th grade: *The Lion the Witch and the Wardrobe*, by C.S. Lewis. 5th graders identify readily with the characters.

6th grade: *Norse Gods and Giants*, by P. and I. d'Aulaire. The new names, settings, and particularly Lokl's trickery enthrall 6th graders.

7th grade: *The Legend of Sleepy Hollow*, by Washington Irving. Male and female literary tastes diverge at this age, but this story appeals to both boys and girls.

8th grade: *Tales of Mystery and Imagination*, by E. A. Poe. A sure fire success in my experience.

9th grade: *Beauty and the Beast*. This story, honoring virtue over physical beauty and dwelling as it does on bodily changes, is particularly appealing to adolescents.

10th grade: *The Man that Corrupted Hadleyburg*, by Mark Twain. Already familiar with Tom Sawyer and Huckleberry Finn, 10th graders welcome more Twain.

11th grade: *Silas Marner*, by George Eliot. Because this story is short, some people mistakenly think it is simple. It sparks intense discussion of personal values.

12th grade: *Childhood, Boyhood and Youth*, by Leo Tolstoy. Many high school students are afraid of Tolstoy, thinking him a difficult, dry writer. This sets them straight.

4.

VOCABULARY GAMES
AND ACTIVITIES

A rich supply of words permits a listener or reader to understand shades of meaning and increases a speaker's or writer's chances of expressing his thoughts exactly. But trying to accumulate vocabulary by memorizing word lists results in a superficial acquaintance. In order to be absorbed, new words must "hover at the rim of the student's experience."*

The vocabulary games and activities in this section are primarily to enhance the development of receptive language even though some of them will give expressive language a workout as well. They are designed to help a student increase his vocabulary of everyday words while learning to file, chart, and organize the vocabulary he already knows. Many students have bigger vocabularies than they realize. Organization can quicken expression since words stored in categories are easier to retrieve than ones which are dropped in a mental grab bag. For example, seventeen first graders who were asked for words about weather started with the predictable: sunny, cold, hot, but with some encouragement the group moved on eagerly to: damp, muggy, icy, foggy, misty, crunchy, and snow-silent.

*quotation from Aylett Cox's address to the Orton Society Conference in New York City in 1979

FUZZY, FURRY, FUNNY

Purpose: accumulation of adjectives
Level of Difficulty: * ** ***
Number of Participants: a whole class or a small group
Materials Required: a familiar object to pass around, one posterboard and notebook ring per object, index cards or slips of paper, and simple drawing materials
Time Required: 30 minutes per session
Description: Start by passing a familiar object around the room. Ask each student to look at it, feel it, and find a single word to describe it. A group of third graders, given a Paddington Bear wearing a blue jacket, rain hat, and boots produced: cute, soft, cuddly, pretty, nice, friendly, woofy, fuzzy, hairy, dressed, and stuffed. A twelfth-grade group given the same Paddington said: cute, soft, cuddly, loveable, mythical, fanciful, synthetic, rain-proofed, Gloucester-fishermanesque, glass-eyed, opaque, heart-warming, and appealing.

As the object is passed from person to person and each one gives a descriptive word, the teacher writes each adjective on the posterboard and also on a slip of paper. When the number of words equals the number of students, each student picks a slip of paper and must use the adjective in a sentence to describe something other than the familiar object. (Examples: A rabbit is as fuzzy as Paddington.) Each student writes out and illustrates his sentence and reads it aloud. The group of illustrated sentences is collected on the notebook ring and displayed on a bulletin board along with the poster containing the adjectives and the object.

When the group has practiced with a tangible object, see how they respond to a word. "Sweater" prompted the following: soft, pretty, attractive, expensive, cashmere, shetland, orlon, knitted, flexible, tubular, portable, shrinkable, protective, dressy, sporty, thin, bulky, cabled, packable, smooth, nubby, scratchy. Although this list is hardly startling in its profundity or originality, its context makes it heartening. It came from a group of ninth grade girls whose spoken comments on clothing had been restricted almost entirely to two phrases, " 's nice" and " 's gross." Each of the collected adjectives was a familiar word to each girl but had remained in a distant mental file.

If you have have space leave the adjective posters out where your students can see them. You will begin to hear the words in conversation and see them in composition.

READY, SET, GO

Purpose: accumulation of verbs
Level of Difficulty: *   **   ***
Number of Participants: whole class or small group
Materials Required: 1 posterboard per action
Time Required: 15–30 minutes per session
Description: The teacher chooses an action and asks the group to describe it in as many ways as possible. For example, a second grader, asked to describe the many ways a human being moves, said: walk, hop, run, skip, jump, leap, skate, slide, ski, twirl, bounce, jog, sprint, swim, scissor-kick, wiggle, dance, roll, stamp. You could ask how animals move (gallop, slither, soar), or cars.

As in the previous game, when an action has been chosen, the teacher writes each suggested verb on both the posterboard and an index card. When the number of verbs is equal to the number of students, ask each participant to pick a card and make up and illustrate posterboard. Here are three examples: "How does an sentences on the notebook ring and hang it beside the poster in the classroom or the hall.

QUICKLY, QUIETLY

Purpose: accumulation of adverbs
Level of Difficulty: * ** ***
Number of Participants: a small group or a whole class
Materials Required: one posterboard per action.
Time Required: 15–30 minutes per session
Description: The procedure is the same as it is for the previous two games. The teacher chooses an action and asks the group to describe it in as many ways as possible, and writes the accumulated words on the posterboard. Here are three examples: "How does an animal move?" Quietly, noisily, sneakily, stealthily energetically, lazily, fast, gracefully, sinuously, awkwardly. "How do people eat?" Noisily, quietly, fast, slowly, greedily, gratefully, hungrily, politely. "How does a student learn?" Eagerly, grudgingly, reluctantly, joyfully.

SMILE

Purpose: accumulation of simile and figures of speech
Level of Difficulty: * ** ***
Number of Participants: small group or whole class
Materials Required: a list of similes and figures of speech on a poster (see below)
Time Required: 30 minutes per session
Description: Before we can ask children to develop simile as an expressive skill or to use figures of speech, we must be sure they do not misunderstand them. Some children with limited abstract language ability are physically uncomfortable with such descriptions as: open-minded, golden-hearted, cold-blooded, or sharp-eyed. Such a child will not say "you crack me up," and he will not "get a kick out of you." On your poster write all the old stand-bys you and the group can remember. Here are some samples:

quick as a wink
cold as ice
good as gold
fresh as a daisy
deadly as poison
noisy as a cageful of monkeys
swift as a deer
spinning like a top
slow as molasses in January
trembling like a leaf
roaring like a lion
high as a kite
fast as the wind
eats like a pig
bounces like a ball
cold as charity
hard as Pharaoh's heart
raining like cats and dogs
rare as a blue moon
frequent as a month of Sundays

When you have as many phrases as you have group members, ask each student to choose one and draw a picture illustrating its meaning. Write the phrase on the back of the paper, pass the pictures around, and see if the group can supply the correct phrase for the picture. Remind your students to illustrate the real meaning of the phrase. You aren't looking for pictures of rainstorms with cats and dogs falling out of the sky.

POLES APART

Purpose: accumulation of opposites
Level of Difficulty: *   **   ***
Number of Participants: pairs, small groups, or brainstorm with a whole class
Materials Required: *Bingo* paper and tokens or cards for *Old Maid* or *Concentration*

Time Required: 20–30 minutes
Description: Choose *Bingo*, *Old Maid*, or *Concentration* and play accordingly. Here are some sample word lists:

* *early level*
  hot / cold
  white / black
  straight / curvy
  kind / mean
  hungry / full

** *intermediate*
  strange / familiar
  absent / present
  dangerous / safe
  come / go
  borrow / lend

** *more advanced*
  ebb / flow
  stale / fresh
  obscure / obvious
  invite / repel
  fetter / release

*** *fancy*
  dominant / subservient
  gracious / churlish
  limpid / turbid
  palatable / distasteful
  encumber / extricate

GOING, GOING, GONE

Purpose: practice with present and past tenses
Level of Difficulty: * ** ***
Number of Participants: pairs, small groups, or brainstorm with a whole class
Materials Required: *Bingo* paper and tokens or cards for *Old Maid* or *Concentration*

Time Required: 20–30 minutes
Description: Choose *Bingo*, *Old Maid*, or *Concentration* and
play accordingly. Here are some sample word lists:

* *early level*	** *harder*
is / was	have / had
am / was	run / ran
sit / sat	cry / cried
do / did	wobble / wobbled
go / went	miss / missed

*** *common errors*

catch / caught   (not catched)
buy / bought   (noy buyed)
teach / taught   (not teached)
think / thought   (not thinked)
bring / brought   (not brang)

SYN

Purpose: accumulation of synonyms
Level of Difficulty: **   ***   ****
Number of Participants: pairs, small groups, or brainstorm
    with a whole class
Materials Required: *Bingo* paper and tokens or *Old Maid* or
    Concentration cards
Time Required: 20 or 30 minutes
Description: Choose *Bingo*, *Old Maid*, or *Concentration* and
play accordingly. Here are some sample word lists:

** *intermediate verbs*

have / own
eat / munch
pretend / make believe
yell / holler
wiggle / squirm

*** *more advanced verbs*

gladden / delight
influence / sway
restore / renew
hit / slug
declare / proclaim

**** *fancy verbs*

placate / pacify
divest / dismantle
eject / oust
vilify / malign
swerve / deviate

** *intermediate adjectives*

hard / difficult
tasty / delicious
sad / gloomy
neat / tidy
happy / cheerful

** *more advanced adjectives*

gigantic / colossal
regal / kingly
unique / sole
fatigued / weary
juvenile / youthful

ROOTS

Purpose: recognizing roots
Level of Difficulty: *   **   ***
Number of Participants: pairs, small groups, or brainstorm
with a whole class
Materials Required: *Bingo* paper and tokens or cards for *Old
Maid* or *Concentration*

Time Required: 20–30 minutes per session
Description: Choose your game format and play accordingly.
   Here are some sample word lists:

  * love / loving
    catch / catcher
    fine / finest
    two / twice
    lock / unlock

 ** demo = people / democracy
    tele = far / telephone or telescope
    micro = small / microscope
    amor = love / amorous
    pre = before / preview

*** bellum = war
    gero = bear   belligerent / warlike

    arth = joint
    itis = inflammation   arthritis / painful joints

    geo = earth
    graph = write   geography / earth written down

    thermo = temperature
    meter = measure   thermometer / temperature-measure

    lepra = rough, scaly
    ist = one who   lepidopterist / one who studies insects

Affix and Root Cards (Educator's Publishing Service, 75 Moulton St. Cambridge, Mass.) is an invaluable source of new words and useful as an umpire for disputes. Charting Greek and Latin roots, the set is inexpensive, durable, and helpful to anyone interested in etymology.
   Do not feel bound by a game format. Brainstorming to see how many pairs a group can accumulate produces excellent results.

HOMONYMBLE

Purpose: practice with homographs

Level of Difficulty: ** ***

Number of Participants: pairs, small groups, or brainstorm with whole class

Materials Required: *Bingo* paper and tokens or cards for *Old Maid* or *Concentration*.

Time Required: 30 minutes

Description: Decide which game format you want to use and play accordingly

Here is a sample word list:

hear / here
their / there
red / read
write / right
blue / blew
way / weigh
new / knew
steel / steal
meet / meat
air / heir
flew / flue
our / are

triples:

to / two / too
vain / vein / vane
so / sew / sow
sent / scent / cent

LOOK ALIKES

Purpose: practice with homographs
Level of Difficulty: **   ***
Number of Participants: pairs, small groups, or brainstorm
    with a whole class
Materials Required: cards for *Old Maid* or *Concentration*.
    Note that there are some triples. See specifics below.
Time Required: 30 minutes
Description: Homographs are words with the same spelling
    but with different meanings and sometimes different
    pronunciations. There is the *bow* of a ship, a boy or an
    actress learns to make a *bow*. A little girl may wear a
    bow in her hair but it will be different from a violinist's
    bow. Like homonyms, homographs lend themselves
    easily to *Old Maid* or *Concentration* in which the players
    accumulate either pairs or triples. In order to score a
    point the player must give sentences using each word
    correctly in its different ways. Here is a sample word list:

    saw (eyes) / saw (wood)
    hose (fire) / hose (stockings)
    bill (bird) / bill (dollar)
    wind (blow) / wind (a ball of string)
    fly (by flapping of wings) / fly (as a passenger)
    present (to give) / present (a gift)
    content (replete) / content (what's inside)
    admit (confess) / admit (let in)
    absorbing (engrossing) / absorbing (sponge-like)
    forego (precede) / forgo (abstain)
    prevent (precede) / prevent (impede)

    draw (a picture) / draw (a gun) / draw (a card)
    run (go) / run (in a stocking) / run (baseball)
    table (in a kitchen) / table (to delay) / table (a
      schedule)

pound (with a hammer) / pound (a weight) / pound (money)

right (correct) / right (not left) / right (to set straight)

Encourage your students to accumulate additional combinations.

SKI LIFT

Purpose: reinforcing comprehension of confusing words and phrases

Level of Difficulty: * ** ***

Number of Participants: 2–4

Materials Required: game board (see below), die, and one pawn per player

Time Required: 20–30 minutes.

Description: Use a manila file folder to make the game board. Tape an envelope on the outside which will hold a master card containing sample sentences. Draw the game path on the inside.

Outside

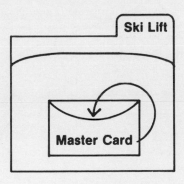

Open the folder and draw a path with thirty-three spaces. On three of the spaces put hazards or obstacles; on thirty spaces put the words you wish to practice.

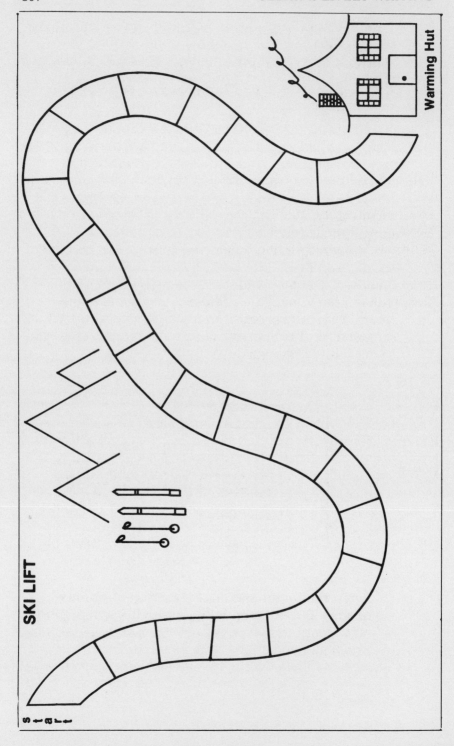

1. Sample word list: unless, until, but, when, then, if, what, because, by, near, at, around, around ten o'clock, from, from three until four, on, on Sunday before, in case, whenever, between, among, so, after, since, although, perhaps, each, every other, column, row.

2. The hazards could be: broken binding ... go back two spaces, boiler plate ... you fell down ... go back three spaces, free lift ticket ... advance two spaces.

3. Write sentences using each word or phrase on a Master Card. A player who has trouble using a word may consult it. It is, in effect, his ski lift. In turn, each player rolls the die, moves his pawn the appropriate number of spaces, and must use the word he lands on in a sentence. The first player to reach the warming hut is the winner.

BLACK AND BLUE

Purpose: categorizing and color-coding the language of math word problems and following directions

Level of Difficulty: ** ***

Number of Participants: whole class or small groups

Materials Required: 4 pieces of white posterboard and 4 colored pens (black, green, red, blue)

Time Required: 15–30 minutes to write each poster, short times for review, additions or sprints thereafter

Description: Label the four posters as follows: In black ink write the heading Directions, in green write Increase, in red Decrease, and in blue Relationships.

Ask your students for some instruction words which are used in giving directions or instructions. Write them on the poster headed Directions, using the black pen. They may suggest such terms as "count" and "underline". Follow a similar procedure and color-code the vocabulary of the other categories. Here are some sample word lists:

Directions (black): list, circle, underline, cross out, fill in, dot, enter, measure, count, graph, at the top, in the corner, left, right, upper, lower, column, row.

Increase (green): add, multiply, times, increase, enlarge, augment, product, larger, greater, more, sum, total, area.

Decrease (red): subtract, divide, the difference between, decrease, minimize, diminish, smaller, less, fewer.

Relationships (blue): ratio, :: (analogy), degree —er, —est, greater than, smaller than, interval.

Leave the posters on display and add new words as your students think of them. When everyone is familiar with the vocabulary, categories, and color-coding, play a sudden-death elimination drill in which you call a term and the student replies with the name of the appropriate color. Teacher: "total", Student: "green". A student who answers incorrectly or hesitates beyond the established time limit is eliminated and must then write the term in the appropriate color. The survivor is the winner.

Many students whose computation is accurate are not sure which arithmetical process is called for by certain words, and their math suffers accordingly. Familiarity with this vocabulary allows the student to concentrate on the mathematics instead of the English.

PART II.

Practice

5.

EXPRESSIVE LANGUAGE: Gesture, Speaking, and Writing

Expressive language flows from a pool, spring-fed by listening and reading. It is the medium for confluence with other living people or with posterity, the vessel for information, and the faucet for original thought. The greater the depth of the speaker's or writer's vocabulary, the greater his chances of clear expression. Seven-year-old Carlie is able to explain that she doesn't want to go to the Milner's house because she is afraid of their big dog, while her little sister, just learning to talk, can only clutch her Mother's skirt and whimper.

All people need to be able to make statements and formulate questions. Many students will venture beyond factual expression to narrative and poetry, and a few will develop eloquence.

Most children welcome a chance to let their imaginations loose on paper, and they enjoy playing with different kinds of expression. Some few, after practicing and polishing, will combine force with fluency. A great writer will invent memorable metaphors as T.S. Eliot did in describing a constricted life as one measured out in coffee spoons.

Six overlapping levels of expressive language traditionally cited in language texts form the framework for the following games and activities. Each overlapping level has its own glories, hazards, and stoppers, and since the language levels work in constant interplay, problems in any one are more likely to overflow than remain isolated. To teach writing, we must understand how each one of the six levels works and what happens if it is insufficiently developed.

The first level is *gesture*, used by people of all ages to express many kinds of emotion. There is no mistaking the happiness in a baby's smiling, wiggling response to a returning parent, or the threat of tumult in the imperious stamping of a two-year-old foot. Nor is gesture limited to childlike communication; a lascivious wink says "I dare you" without words, and it is easy to read discouragement in the weary shrug of a spouse's shoulder.

A child who does not use gesture for communication (or who is reluctant to make eye contact through which gesture can be emphasized) may be in serious physical or emotional trouble and should have a thorough physical examination. On the other side of the same coin, a child or adult who consistently uses gesture in place of words may also be in trouble. He may be unable to remember words when he needs them, as we will see when we consider labels.

Labels, the second level, allow a child to name his world. Once he has a name for a person or a thing, he can summon it whenever necessary. As Selma Fraiberg points out in *The Magic Years*, a baby learns that "Mama" is a symbol for a key figure in his life. When he is put to bed and is heard chanting her name, he does not need to call her physically to his side because he has learned to bring her back mentally by saying her name. Labels, then, are keys of access, retrieval, and sorting, although a child may label and sort differently from an adult.

Morgan adores his grandmother who is a heavy smoker. One day when he was four years old his father took him on a September outing to the beach. They had the whole stretch to themselves . . . soft sand, sparkling sky and water, a dream come true of clean, clear purity. The child, who had been strolling independently, all of a sudden ran back to his father's side triumphantly holding a clam shell. "Look, Daddy, look! An ashtray!"

"Thing-a-ma-jig", "and um", "like -uh", and "ya know" are the crutches of a child or adult who has trouble remembering labels and retrieving words. Although he knows what he wants to say, the necessary word floats somewhere just beyond his grasp. Several years ago novelty shops sold a fortune-predictor called the *Magic 8 Ball*, a round black glass filled with black liquid. It had a flat spot on the bottom so it could rest on a table, and at the top there was a square clear window. You were supposed to pick up the *Magic 8 Ball*, ask a vital question ("Will Harry invite me to the movies?"), tip it around, and then wait for the answer to float to the window. As the words approached through the murky liquid you could tell whether the answer would be long or short, but the actual words remained clouded until the last moment. Finally the message would touch the window. Instantly and clearly you could read "Yes", "Chances Doubtful", "Don't Give up", or "Your wish will not be granted".

In conversation most of us roll our mental *Magic 8 Ball* constantly and unconsciously. Words float to the window of our minds, arriving with clear contours and on time. The dysnomic or aphasic person is not that lucky. It is as though his *Magic 8-Ball* is filled with more and murkier ink and his window made of rippled glass. He must squint, wait, and stall for time. In searching for the elusive name of an object, he may invent a descriptive term: a hinge becomes a "doorswinger," a sock a "footmiten," or a spindle a "roller-thingy." While he is groping for the name of a person, place, or thing, the absense of his target word creates what Harvard linguist Anthony Bashir calls "an intensely active gap" that no substitute can really fill. When "Hammurabi" or "Mt. Monadnock" finally floats into view, the relief is as specific and intense as a good sneeze.

As people mature they develop compensations and disguise their difficulties. The dysnomic person will choose safe conversational territory with a highly familiar vocabulary and his trouble will remain camouflaged as long as he is choosing the topic, but elicited expression, spoken or written, will expose it.

The third level, *connected speech*, describes (red ball), narrates (car go), or expresses desire (Mommy come). Without description we would need a separate word for every object in our past, present, and future. Mastery of our language would require an exhausting number of individual labels. Adjectives, adverbs, prepositions, and markers of time and space allow us to distinguish "the little yellow ball under the chair in the corner" from "the big beach ball on the porch."

The student who has trouble retrieving single labels faces extended difficulty in connected speech. de Hirsch has given us the term "clutterer" to describe someone whose expression is a jumble of empty spots caused by retrieval difficulty and overflow caused by imprecise categorizing and sorting. Although the

clutterer's output may be voluminous, it will be full of circum-
locutions, hesitations, fillers, shifts in sequence, confused organization, and telescoped words. The speaker frequently has trouble
getting to the point. Third-grade Carol's description of making
pancakes is a perfect example.

"It was so good . . . we had them."

"How?"

"Well (long pause) we put it in that bowl, and then, you see,
my sister used one of those things—my grandmother has one—
she keeps it in her house in—well, you know where there's that
pond and those buttons, I mean berries, Um.m.m. . .?"

"Your sister stirred the pancake batter?"

"Oh, oh yes, but this one blop of it got on her dress, her
new dress—it was Sunday—for church and everything—and she
didn't know what to do."

"Did your Mother put the batter on the griddle?"

"Yes, and it made these funny sounds and got all like
bubbles on top until you could turn them over, but the dog
didn't eat his—and we weren't late. They were soooooo good
with all that um, um, sticky on top of them."

Volume, yes. Precision, no. Meanwhile good luck to Carol in
her new Geography unit. They are working on deserts. Proudly
she said, "I'm going to study the Sandhara."

The fourth level is the use of *morphology*, word endings which
indicate such things as plurals (dog, dogs), size and degree (big,
bigg*er*, bigg*est*), and verb tenses (jump, jump*ing*, jump*ed*).
Morphology is the tool for organizing the frequently confusing
concepts of space and time. The language of size is one
foundation of the language of space: biggest, smallest, tallest or
nearest. Verb tenses establish sequence which is the language of
time. A person who does not sort past, present, and future by
understanding and using verb tenses is a prisoner of the present,
barred from sequenced memory and denied its reciprocal . . .
realistic anticipation.

Mastery of morphology makes way for the development of
categories in which to store, retrieve, and cross-reference objects,
people, emotions, and ideas. We can file them according to their
functions; for example, grouping together things which move.
We can sort according to properties, separating the large from the
small, the man-made from the natural, or the soft from the hard.

We can use subjective judgments in slotting things we consider entertaining, boring, desirable, or distasteful. As the child matures he discovers that objects and experiences can belong to more than one category simultaneously, thus increasing the efficiency and depth of his filing system. Sophisticated abstract thinking requires the ability to make comparisons and see relationships. To the existence of morphology and categories we owe the existence of analogies: Paint:painter :: farmer:farmer; mouse:mice :: die:dice; biggest:smallest :: loudest:quietest; walked:walking :: ate:eating. Without categories, ideas and experiences would simply fall into our heads in a mental Mulligan Stew. The child or adult who has not learned to notice morphological markers in listening and speaking will not notice them in reading and therefore will not write them.

The fifth level, the use of *syntax*, governs the order of words and structure of sentences, allowing the speaker to convert a declarative statement to a question (The panther has escaped. Has the panther escaped?) and to connect several thoughts together in one sentence (The red ball the boy was chasing fell in the well) as opposed to the less mature "You know that ball . . . the red one? Well, this boy was chasing it, and it went down this big hole.) Syntax, like morphology, is an organizer. Without it labels, descriptions, sequences, and sizes all jumble together like a washing-machine load of family laundry.

Leontine was a delicate first-grade girl. Meticulously groomed, and eager to be precise, she had tremendous difficulty learning to formulate a question. She would inquire of her teacher, "Where they are?" or "What this is?" The symptom seemed isolated. However, closer investigation revealed large pockets of confusion at earlier language levels. For example, she had heard of "big, bigger, biggest" and nodded politely when asked if she understood them. But when trying to express those ideas herself, she said "big", smiled, and gestured with her hands. She was confused when she tried to slot tenses of verbs into categories of "yesterday, today, and tomorrow." "Today" was secure, but the other two blended into "maybe." Difficulty in forming questions, the audible symptom of her difficulty, was the tip of her problem, not the base. Her understanding of morphology was weak, she had grievous trouble with verb tenses, and many labels eluded her.

Semantics, the sixth level, separates sense from nonsense. Endings and order are worthless in the absence of meaning. In *The Dragons of Eden* Carl Sagan tells the story of an apocryphal computer capable of translating English into Chinese. At a demonstration an experimenter fed it the saying "out of sight, out of mind" and received in return a paper bearing some Chinese characters. To test the accuracy of the translation, he fed the Chinese characters back into the machine which produced a technically accurate but meaningless translation, turning "out of sight, out of mind" into "invisible idiot."

Like making a cake, semantics allows the user to blend individual ingredients into a new and complete whole. It changes the flour of labels, the butter of description, the milk of connected words, the egg whites of morphology, and the spice of syntax into angel food or devil's food as the case may be. This final level, semantic skill, is the highest kind of verbal expression, but not everyone is capable of enjoying abstraction. Metaphor, simile, riddles, symbolic poetry and analogy are gourmet fare which the concrete or limited thinker cannot digest.

Here are two precepts for teaching expressive language at all six levels. First, expose your students to conversation, using words as vessels for thought and companions of reason. This may be a new experience for those who are only accustomed to hearing words of exhortation (hurry up!) and prohibition (stop it!).

Last spring a father and mother arranged a conference with their oldest child's teacher. Ed, a fourth grader, was having trouble controlling his impulsive behavior in school. His classroom participation and his written work were unfocused and, although his arithmetic and reading were mechanically correct, he couldn't solve word problems and his comprehension was weak. There were two other boys in the family: Chuckie, who was having trouble on the kindergarten playground because he often hit the other children, and an eleven-month-old crawler named Joey. In the course of the conference some family patterns emerged: the radio was always playing when the family rode in the car; Ed and Chuckie ate supper earlier than their parents, frequently watching T.V. as they ate; the boys had separate bedrooms; neither parent was in the habit of reading aloud. The baby was usually asleep when the two older boys returned from school and, since that was their Mother's soap opera time, the boys were expected to be quiet in the house or, preferably, to go outside and play. As the conference progressed, Joey explored the room. When he would go too far in any direction his Mother, without explanation, would pick him up like a turtle and turn him around.

No wonder Ed interrupts in class. He is a stranger to the exchange of conversation, and his lack of exposure guarantees sparse, inadequate output. Predictably, Chuckie punches on the playground. These children have no experience in using words to mediate plans and emotions. Their impoverishment is not financial. They live in a large house in an expensive section of their community. Their cars are new and fully equipped, their clothing fashionable, and the boys' athletic equipment is the newest and finest available. Yet these three boys suffer from malnutrition in their daily language diet.

The second precept is that the teacher must give the student experiences to describe and reinterpret symbolically. Having learned to understand the symbolism of incoming words and to generate imagery through listening and reading, the student must now symbolize the non-present through speaking and writing. Remember this analogy:

receptive language:expressive language :: experience:description.

Chapter 6 explores *Problems Particular to Writing and How to Minimize Them: Mechanics, Language Disability, and Problems of Approach*. Chapters 7, 8, and 9 offer three steps to developing and expanding expressive language. Chapter 7, *Build a Bannister: Frameworks for Speaking, Prose and Poetry*, offers patterns for the student to hold. The activities revolve around a common experience, an object, or a group of words. Chapter 8, *Word Games and Word Patterns*, offers opportunities for the student to play with words. Chapter 9, *Stimulate and Stand Back: Models and Experiments for Factual, Persuasive, and Aesthetic Writing* exposes the student to models, methods, or concepts and encourages him to create his own examples. As the back-to-basics movement gathers momentum we would do well to remind ourselves and our students of a truth expressed by Charlene Lowry in an article titled *Poetry for Basics**—"the most basic skill of all is the ability to create."

* *Educational Leadership*, Journal of the Association for Supervision and Curriculum Development, December, 1978.

6.

PROBLEMS PARTICULAR TO WRITING AND WAYS TO MINIMIZE THEM: Mechanics, Language Disability, and Problems of Approach

I am an optimist by nature and also know through research and experience that the activities in this book are successful in teaching students to write. However it would be unfair to teachers and their students to gloss over problems and disabilities which are particular to writing. Pretending that they do not exist will not make them go away. When a student or a teacher says, "I've tried, but this writing still isn't any good," it is important to determine what isn't any good: the appearance of the paper, the handwriting, the spelling, the vocabulary, the rhythm, or the organization. Poor quality in any of these is enough to create an overall appearance of weakness, frustrating to student and teacher alike.

This is not the place for a treatise on the diagnosis and treatment of learning disabilities, but as teachers we will do our jobs better if we understand the particular difficulties which can undermine written expression. Once acquainted with these specific problems we will recognize them and be able to call them by name when we run into them. Understanding the nature of the problem is the first step to solving it.

Mechanical problems with handwriting, spelling, and punctuation can cripple, undermine, or confuse written work. Underlying language confusion, which is not evident in conversation, may sap strength from prose or prompt errors which startle the teacher's eye and create an erroneous impression of stupidity. The lurking disabilities of residual dyslexia and word-retrieval difficulty (dysnomia) are real, painful to the student, and unacknowledged in most books and courses on the teaching of writing. These problems do not evaporate; neither does the student outgrow them spontaneously. The student needs the specific kinds of help and teaching which are suggested in this chapter.

In other cases, poor written work is produced by students who are disinclined, discouraged, disorganized, or whose prose is distended. Though not disabled, they too need help. This chapter suggests ways to dissipate their problems, which may be isolated or may overlap with one another.

MECHANICAL PROBLEMS

Handwriting. Ideally there is a comfortable equilibrium between the production of thought and the mechanics of handwriting. But a student may struggle with penmanship because he has trouble remembering how to form letters, or he may know how he wants to form them but his pencil behaves like a saboteur rather than an ally. A student may remember how to form the shapes he needs but have trouble fitting them into the alotted spaces on the paper, causing his writing to be cramped or scrawly: *p*, *g*, *q*, and *y* may float above the line as though filled with helium; *h,n,i,l,t*, and *b* may be the same height; *r* may be indistinguishable from *v*; there may be inadequate spaces between words or exaggerated gaps inside them. Or if a writer has a tense or improper pencil grip, his hand may tire easily in which case writing becomes physically exhausting.

The student who has to struggle with crippled handwriting has little attentional energy left over for concepts, imagination, or enjoyment, with the result that his papers are either tidy with poor content or his good ideas are messily presented. His instinct for self-preservation may lead him to make his words, sentences, paragraphs, and narratives as brief as possible, like the fourth grader whose composition read:

My Cat
I like my cat. My cat is black.
She is nice.
The End

His output will be sparse, sterile, and disappointing. In the second case, where the writer's mechanical skills don't keep pace with the flow of ideas, he may unwittingly omit words or whole phrases with a predictable distortion of sense. Remember the third grader in the introduction who, in the grip of retelling *Snow White*, was in such a rush to get to the climax that she omitted two key words, "angry at," and wrote distortedly, "the queen was the princess."

Here are some suggestions: first, encourage your students to form large letters. They are easier to make and read than small ones and easier to connect with one another in cursive script. Students from the third grade up who still ought to write large letters because of their lagging fine-motor development are apt to think big handwriting is babyish. To ward off such embarrassment give bonuses for jumbo work.

Second, many school systems teach printing in kindergarten through second grades, and introduce cursive writing in third. If he has learned cursive require him to use it instead of printing. Handwriting that connects letters is easier for a dysgraphic student than handwriting which isolates them, and the fact that spaces occur between words rather than within them will help him make his work legible and visually attractive.

Third, if the student is ten or older, suggest that he learn to type. Two excellent programs which he can use at home are:

Type It, by Joan Duffy. (Educator's Publishing Service, 75 Moulton St., Cambridge, MA. 02138)

Typing Keys to the Remediation of Reading and Spelling Difficulties, by Maetta Davis. (Academic Therapy Publications, San Raphael, CA. 94901)

Both are available by mail, both publishers will send a catalogue upon request.

Spelling. How to teach spelling is a book in itself. An analysis of errors and how to correct them is another. However, no treatment of writing skills and disabilities would be complete without a spelling section, so without attempting to be comprehensive, I would like to bring out some diagnostic distinctions and offer some practical suggestions.

Spelling words fall into four major categories:

words which are phonetically regular (run)
words which are irregular and must be memorized (one)
words which are governed by rule (running, it's, principle)
words which are connected by their roots (do, does) or
distinguished by their meanings (pedal, peddle)
  peddle)

Poor spellers fall into similar categories. There are those who do not analyze sounds. They tangle the sequence (writing *lats* for *last*) and omit or transpose syllables (writing *rember* for *remember* or *aminal* for *animal*). This is a hard problem to overcome, but if you have such a student suggest that he speak his words before writing them, stretching out the sounds, and writing one syllable at a time.

There are those whose visual memory for word shapes is not crisp. They may use the right letters and appropriate sounds but arrange them incorrectly (writing *freind* or *furend* for *friend*). They are more apt to rely on the sequence of sounds than the sequence of letters. They may spell by trying to reproduce the visual configuration of a word but miss because of inaccurate visual memory (writing *riht* for *right*). This, too, is a difficult problem to overcome. It is reassuring to both students and teachers that 85 percent of the words in our language are regular. Thus only 15 percent are sight words which must be memorized.

There are those who are unfamiliar with spelling rules. In some cases the rules have not been taught, in other cases they didn't sink in. This problem is easier to overcome than the previous two but errors may continue to appear in spontaneous work long after a student has learned to spell the words correctly by rule in isolation. Confusion over when to double a consonant, how to use an apostrophe, and what ending to choose accounts for such a large percentage of common spelling errors that a quick review of these rules seems appropriate here.

Teach your students to double the final consonant when adding a suffix to a one-syllable short vowel word ending in a single consonant. *Example:* run, runner, running. Double the last consonant of a syllable containing a short vowel which is to be followed by consonant-1-e. *Example:* dribble and fiddle as opposed to bridle and rifle.

Explain how apostrophes denote ownership or contractions. The first kind is easy to place correctly if you revere ownership.

The apostrophe follows the possessor or the possessors regardless of a final s.

> *Examples* for singular and plural possession.
> *The cat.* I will warm the cat's milk.
> *The cats.* I will warm the cats' milk.
> *The possessor.* The possessor's privilege is to spend his money. (He has the dollars and he gets the apostrophe too.)
> *The possessors.* The possessors' obligation is to disburse wealth wisely.
> *Charles.* Charles' allowance is skimpy. (Correct.) Charles's allowance is skimpy. (Correct.) Charleses allowance is skimpy (Incorrect.)
> *A fine family.* Jim and Waldo Jones' library is cozy. Jim and Waldo Jones's library is cozy. Jim's and Waldo's library is cozy. The Joneses (there are five of them) sit around in there a lot. All of the Joneses' cars are German. Pretty swell apples, those Joneses!

Apostrophes which mark contractions are easy to place correctly simply by remembering what got squeezed out. The apostrophe marks the spot of the missing letter.

is not	isnot	isn't
I will	Iwill	I'll
they are	theyare	they're

and so forth

Warning! Spell such words with your language sense and your eyes. "You're ears wont help you."

Two generalizations will help your student choose between the endings *le* and *al*, or *us* and *ous*. Usually *us* denotes a noun and *ous* an adjective: It is joyous at the circus. Usually *le* denotes a noun and *al* an adjective: That is the principal principle. If you would like to learn more such generalizations here are four books published by Educator's Publishing Service, 75 Moulton St., Cambridge, MA. 02138, available by mail:

Recipe for Reading, by Nina Traub and *Word Attack Manual*, by Josephine Rudd are good for the adult student, classroom teacher, or resource teacher.

Situation Spelling, by Aylett Cox and *Remedial Techniques for*

Reading, Writing, and Spelling, by Anna Gillingham are excellent reference books for teachers of disabled students but are hard going for the teacher or student who is unfamiliar with the terminology.

Those students who are confused by the structure of language will produce mirror-images of their perplexities in their spelling. Thus the student who doesn't see the pattern of root words may write *dus* and *dewing* for *does* and *doing*. Practice in adding suffixes and prefixes to root words will help alleviate such a problem. Students who have confusion over homonyms will write such perplexing aberrations as *go pedal you're wears* for *go peddle your wares*. Here are two ways to help students avoid homonym errors. First teach them to spell with their language sense to avoid confusing such words as

they're/there/their; your/you're; wear/ware/where.

Second, teach them to learn one word of each pair thoroughly by sight, sound, and sense. When half the pair is secure, process of elimination takes care of the other half. Already the job is reduced by 50%. They should memorize the half they are most likely to write, for example, a medical student might choose *pain*, a carpenter *pane* (unless he was in the habit of hitting his thumb), a baker would use *piece*, the Secretary of State *peace* and so forth. Here is a sample exercise to offer your students.

> I'm glad to here your going to meat me at they're house. I don't no if I'll be on thyme but I'll try. I can find wear they live unless I through out the directions.

Consult Chapter 4 (page 78) for a list of words and games to help learn homonyms.

Those students who misinterpret common labels and sayings reveal their confusion through their spelling, producing malapropisms. Urge such students only to use expressions they really understand and have seen in written form because *in all good consciousness, you can't leave them on tender hooks!*

Those students who have acquired sloppy spelling habits frequently have trouble with the words listed below. Relearning them correctly is a relatively minor task. Simply seeing the list will be enough in some cases. Other students will have to study and memorize. Misspelling these words is common in first and second grade, but the longer the habit continues the harder it is to eradicate.

W words

want
won't
went
were
wear
we're
where
what
when
why and
who

is words

is, am, are, isn't, aren't

do words

do, does, done

go words

go, goes, gone.

One final comment on spelling: keep the whole subject in proportion. Many brilliant people never outgrow bad spelling; they just disguise their problem. School years are indeed painful. But by the time a student reaches high school or college he can enlist a hawk-eyed friend as a proofreader. Later a secretary may take over formal correspondence, and finally a dictionary can become a true friend. Don't, however, tell a confused second grader to "look it up". If he already knew enough about the word to look it up, he wouldn't be in trouble!

Punctuation. Teach punctuation through the ears not the eyes, and cast periods, commas, and capitals in the metaphor of traffic signals. Periods represent stops and are similar to red lights.

Commas indicate pauses and are like orange blinkers signaling pause-and-then-proceed. A capital letter at the beginning of a sentence indicates go. It is an upper case, larger letter to get the sentence going, just the way an extra push on the accelerator is needed to get a vehicle moving again after a full stop. This common sense explanation seems to demystify what is otherwise a bewildering set of rules. Here is a four-step progression of exercises designed to teach accurate simple punctuation.

1. Write out a paragraph with no punctuation marks, and give each student a copy. Read it aloud. Ask the listeners where the stopping points are.

2. Once they have *heard* where the pauses and stops are, ask them to insert the commas, periods, and capitals. Read the paragraph aloud again. Next, give each student a copy of a paragraph in which the periods have been underlined in red, the commas in orange, and the capitals in green. Ask them to read it to themselves, exaggerating the stops and pauses.

3. Ask the student, or group of students, to make up a short paragraph and dictate it to you, indicating stopping points with their voices and telling you which punctuation marks to insert. As the scribe, write the paragraph on the board or an easel for all to see.

4. Finally, ask each student to write and punctuate a short, original paragraph. Remind him to let his ears work for him.

Grading. It is difficult for a teacher to grade the written work of a student who struggles with the kind of mechanical difficulties outlined here. If you face such a situation try this system. Papers which the writer has had time to proofread, copy or type will be graded for mechanics and content together. Papers which are written in class under time pressure (exams, spot quizzes, or spontaneous creative writing assignments) may be graded separately for mechanics and content. This system upholds standards and recognizes the possible discrepancy between mechanical skill and the flow of ideas.

Language Disability. Weak writing may be the result of three invisible language handicaps: insufficient exposure, residual dyslexia, and word-retrieval difficulty. Working singly or in combination they leech vigor from expression. The receptive language activities in the previous section, designed to plant and cultivate for rich language, will help the student who is under-exposed. The problems of disguised dyslexia and word-retrieval difficulty (dysnomia) are subtler, more difficult to overcome, and devastating when they are misunderstood or unacknowledged.

Residual Dyslexia. The writer who struggles with residual dyslexia may camouflage his language confusion by being friendly or garrulous in conversation, and by being able to read.

Initially, it is difficult for the dyslexic to learn the relation-ship between symbols (letters) and sounds, to blend the sounds into words, and to recognize whole words by sight. Thus, starting to read requires fortitude, willingness, and special teaching. But all too often, mastery of decoding is seen as the end of the problem rather than the end of one phase or manifestation. Affability and an air of intelligence may camouflage residual dyslexia, but hiding is not possible in written work which highlights imprecision or latent, unresolved language confusion. Here are some typical errors:

> Subjects and verbs won't agree and the student may write such errors as: *he don't* or *the elephants wasn't.* If your student makes such errors, reteach the concept. It won't arrive by osmosis.
>
> A student who needs to work on plurals, degree, and verb tenses may use these morphological markers incorrectly or omit them entirely, making such errors as: seven clown, biggerer, and last night I jump into bed.

Pronoun confusion is common for these students who may write *sheself* for *herself,* the girls did it *theirself,* or Mrs. Brown asked John to do it *herself. I/me* confusion is pervasive for these students. Here are some samples and quick *I/me* tests:

> *Example.* A third grader:
> "Sarah and me are going to the birthday party."
> *Quick Test.* Repeat the sentence omitting Sarah. Which sounds correct:
>   Me is/are going.
>   I am/are going.
> If a student selects the first, he is not attuned to the sound of

correct English. He needs receptive language work before a series of grammar lessons.

Example. A ninth grader:

Petulant teacher: "Who threw that?"

Honest student: "Me."

Quick Test. Turn the question into a declarative sentence.

Which sounds correct:

Me threw that.

I threw that.

Example. A college sophomore:

"Dear Dad,

Bad news. That exam was too tough. Both Brad and me flunked."

Quick Test. Repeat the sentence leaving only yourself in it. Listen.

Me flunked.

I flunked.

Example. Principal's office:

"You have all expended great hospitality to Ellen and I."

Quick Test. Repeat the sentence leaving Ellen out in the cold.

"You have all extended great hospitality to I."

Never.

Example: Confidantes:

"Just between you and I . . . "

Quick Test. Repeat the phrase replacing *I* and *me* with their plural counterparts *we* and *us*.

"Just between we" is a horror.

"Just between us" makes me sit forward in my chair.

Your students will be delighted to discover the simple trick of being selfish. Explain this additional thing. Some people think that *I* sounds refined and *me* sounds common or uneducated. Vacillators who haven't figured out the way to resolve *I/me* confusion but want to sound suave choose *myself* as a substitute. Like finger-crooking, this verbal ostentation does not convey elegance. "It was kind of Queen Elizabeth to invite Donald and myself to Buckingham Palace" is pretentious as well as inaccurate and the Queen will surely not seek out a boor. Leave *myself* to those who attempt to get on in society, leave Donald behind, and you'll quickly hear whether I or me is correct. *Myself* is correct when used reflexively, for emphasis, or following a preposition: I burned myself. I, myself, think that chocolate is delicious. I bought a sweater for Lucia and one for myself.

Students with language confusion use plural pronouns for singular nouns, writing such errors as: *Everybody* wants *their* paper to be correct instead of *everybody* wants *his* paper to be correct. Or *Each* person wants *their* money back rather than *each* person wants *his* money back. In case of hopeless confusion or panic, teach your students to omit the pronoun and rearrange the words: *Everybody* wants a correct paper. *Each* person is demanding a refund. Many readers would not notice the *everybody/their* error, but those who do will consider the user careless, ignorant, or lacking in fine tuning. Correct usage is crisp, incorrect is soggy and users are treated accordingly. Help your students be crisp.

These students may write sentence fragments instead of sentences, producing such errors as: *Because it was dark.* If you would help such a student, speak to him in complete sentences. Ask him to listen for the difference between a whole and a fragment as you give him some samples. Ask him to reread his work with his ears as well as his eyes.

These students are prey to the embarrassment of malapropisms. The father of a bride-to-be, looking through a batch of responses to the wedding invitations saw: Miss Mary Smith excepts with pleasure. Before passing the letter along to his wife he penciled at the bottom: Maybe she'll get lost in the shovel. The Mary Smiths among our students do not need extra phonics, grammar rules, or crash courses in punctuation. They need more work in language.

Although learning to decode starts the dyslexic student on the road to reading and writing language, just as speaking single words starts the child on the road to expressive competence, beginning a task must not be confused with completing it. After a student has mastered decoding he needs continued exposure to the shadings and nuances of language. The child who was dyslexic initially will need extra help. While his initial difficulty no longer keeps him from reading, we should remember that it was there and watch for its shadow across the pages of his writing.

Dysnomia. The dysnomic writer has trouble with word retrieval. As discussed at some length in the beginning of the expressive language section, word-retrieval problems leave the speaker with an elusive, I've-got-it-on-the-tip-of-the-tongue feeling. In contrast to the person who speaks slowly because he chooses his words with precision, the dysnomic speaker uses fillers (*and—um*), time buyers (*You know what I mean*), gestures (of face or hands), avoidance, or an avalanche of peripheral words as he seeks his target. But these conversational dodges don't work on paper. If the student who is hunting for words must also concentrate on mechanics of handwriting, his dysnomia will be aggravated. Because handwriting is visible and word-retrieval is not, his difficulty may be misinterpreted as being primarily mechanical.

Arthur's teacher was in despair. She knew the child was intellectually aquiver. He read with interest and comprehension, his workbook blanks were filled in correctly, and yet his written work was a disaster. His handwriting sprawled and his papers were Swiss-cheesed with holes from constant frustrated erasures. After a whole hour of working at his desk in a serenely quiet classroom, his story consisted of only one sentence and a fragment. The teacher tried bribery, scolding, a seat facing a blank wall, and a heart-to-heart talk. No improvement. Finally, all the boy's teachers got together to confer. Gradually, like that Magic 8 Ball mentioned in the preceding chapter, through the murky ink an answer floated up.

Arthur's mind was, indeed, crackling with information and ideas. His humor was budding and his emotions were powerful. Because he was bright and interested in so many things his particular disability was not obvious in his conversations or actions. However, his word-retrieval problem, or dysnomia, lurked like a rock ledge hidden by a high tide.

He was reading above grade level, scored in the 98th percentile in receptive vocabulary tests, could answer specific comprehension questions or fill in workbook blanks, and he seemed to have overcome his earlier handwriting difficulties. In other words, when a framework was provided for him, he functioned well. "But," the teacher said, "I'm really confused. Lots of times he'll appear to be listening while other people are talking, I'll think he's with us, but then he'll raise his hand and come up with something completely beside the point." Little did she realize how accurately she described his erratic thought processes.

Dysnomia is an agent of dispersal. Arthur would start with everyone else at point A, heading for point B. The path would seem straight, but along the way some necessary word would slip away. He would try to return to point A to start over, but the necessary word there would elude him, so he would pick a close relative and start off again. Consequently, instead of sharing points A and B with his classmates, his terminals would differ and he would volunteer something "completely beside the point." Drawn on paper, it might look like this:

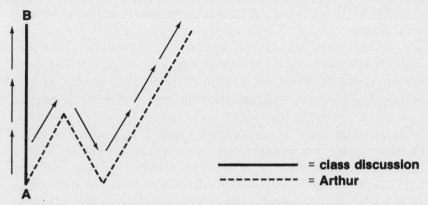

His shimmering supply of ideas made things worse, not better; they provided too many fireflies for him to follow. His handwriting problem, originally thought to be the source of his trouble, actually masked and aggravated it. Words which had been elusive in conversation vanished entirely when he had to concentrate on penmanship. Extemporaneous written work, simultaneously requiring focused attention, mechanical precision, and specific vocabulary, was beyond him.

Dysnomia and its manifestations do not stop at fourth grade. They continue through school, college, and later life. For example, a language diagnostician received permission to study the exam booklets handed in by the twenty students in a college seminar. She had never met or spoken with any of them, but on the basis of their written work she identified three with mild to severe dysnomia. She wrote out hypothetical samples of their speech for their amazed professor, who said he had heard all the same patterns in class discussion but never realized their significance.

How could a student with such a problem attain senior standing in a demanding college? In elementary school the dysnomic is at the mercy of a constantly changing curriculum.

Over and over he is introduced to new vocabulary because each subject matter has its own set. Being bounced from *denominator* to *democracy* to *diphthong* is *disaster* for the *dysnomic*! But in high school the problem abates because vocabularies cling to their disciplines, and at last the student is allowed some choice of subject matter. Still more choice is available in the early years of college, followed by extensive options toward the end. Gradually the student moves to being a selector instead of a sitting duck. The vocabularies of his favorite subjects are not elusive because he uses them all the time. But, when he is pushed into unfamiliar territory or when he must write and think simultaneously under the pressure of time, as in an exam, his former difficulties will usually reappear.

In serious cases the dysnomic writer needs language therapy. In milder cases, try these:

1. Teach as many word associations as possible. Work in such pairs as opposites, homonyms, synonyms and constant companions: hot/cold, meet/meat, humid/moist, comb/brush. A word stored alone has only one handle for retrieval. A word stored in a pair has two. By playing with combinations the student can increase his number of handles geometrically. (See pages 71–92.)

2. Teach and rehearse vocabulary ahead of time. Familiarity with such words as primogeniture, feif, guild, plague, tithe, and serf frees a student to concentrate on the trials of the Middle Ages instead of terminology. Like giving crutches to a student with a sprained ankle, such help provides necessary support. It is not pampering.

3. Teach your student to list needed vocabulary on an index card before he starts to write. Before they become elusive, he can capture the words he needs by consulting the text, his notes, a friend, or a teacher. If he keeps the card handy while he writes, his energies can go into thinking instead of hunting.

4. Give such a student either short factual assignments or ones in which original expression is rewarded. A short project requires a limited number of words. The student can finish before exhaustion aggravates the problem. In fanciful work, the student who cannot remember "mi-

grating flock" and produces "flying wedge" will be rewarded for originality. Assignments which demand length, originality, and precision are the hardest.

PROBLEMS OF APPROACH

Poor writing is not always the result of mechanical difficulties or language deficits and disabilities. The writer may be disinclined, disheartened, disorganized, or one whose compositions are distended.

The Disinclined Writer. Panic sends many a writer into an intricate series of dance steps designed to lead his feet away from the typewriter, the desk, or a piece of clean paper. Writing requires commitment and brings exposure, either of which may generate temporary reluctance or permanent avoidance.

Temporary reluctance produces pencil-sharpening, trips to the bathroom, paper-crumpling, sudden vital errands, lists or telephone calls to be made—innumerable activities in which the frightened writer, abdicating the desk, rushes around trying to bring his environment under his dominion because he lacks sway over his mind and pencil.

In young students and also in adults, avoidance is often an attempt to camouflage lack of confidence. Apprehension can come from a writer's fear of being unable to finish what he starts, from unfamiliarity with writing, or from unwillingness to expose ignorance, inadequate skills or an unpopular point of view. As the student fears failure, the adult fears exposure. A grown person, competent in the skills of living, who looks intelligent and perhaps even athletic, doesn't want to be stripped bare by a piece of paper. Yet no new clothing, loud voice, gruff order, or overhead smash will cover up lack of style or a poor punch line on paper.

The student with this affliction hands assignments in late and seizes every opportunity to give an oral report rather than a written one. The businessman tells his secretary, "Send them a letter thanking them for the order and say we'll see them in Peoria." Those who lack secretaries telephone instead of writing.

However, avoiding the situation simply feeds the phobia. The way to overcome it is to begin. Try this simple and unintimidating way.

Start small. A standard piece of typing paper may look frightening because there is so much space to fill, but no one is afraid of an index card. It feels familiar to any fan who has carried baseball cards, golfer who has recorded a score, anyone who has jotted down directions, or who has made lists. After giving your student a simple topic such as "favorite food," ask him to write one sentence about it on a card. When he is completely comfortable writing one sentence on any given topic, expand to two and then three. Since it is hard to fit three sentences on a small index card, he will need a bigger one. As you ask him for more sentences, he will need more space and will finally reach for a piece of paper. Sentence desensitization is a painless way to get started.

Another way is to ask your student to copy a poem or short passage he enjoys. Even if the thoughts are someone else's, putting them on paper gives the copier a chance to feel a sense of completion. Furthermore, practicing a mechanical skill such as handwriting, which might seem like imprisonment to a focused student, gives a feeling of grounding to one whose concentration is vulnerable to fear.

The Disheartened Writer. The writer who gets negative responses to his work soon reacts with these three R's: retreat, reluctance, refusal.

Ben, who had done poorly in composition all the way through elementary school, was asked to write a ninth-grade science report on the ecology of a salt marsh. Having conceived an original plan, he approached the assignment eagerly. To their amazement, his parents could hear him in his room walking, writing, reaching for books, laughing, and finally typing the finished product. He had written it as a soap opera: intrigue, threat, climax interspersed with, "Tune in tomorrow to see whether the hermit crab will be evicted, penniless, from his hard-won home." Of course, Ben had to have accumulated a thorough understanding of life in the salt marsh before he could convert it to dramatic form. He had studied hard, thought, and joyfully created a script which was entertaining, instructive, and original.

What more could a teacher want? However, his work was returned to him marked:

"*D*. This course is science, not fiction."

If your goal is to teach strong, vivid expression, encourage each link between writing and joy.

The Disorganized Writer. Color and geometry give the writer visual clues for organizing his work. Here are some suggestions for using them.

First, be sure the student understands the five *wh* words (who, what, when, where, why) and the organization they represent. I like to add a sixth, *how*. After all, it has the same letters as *who* in different sequence and, like the others, acts as an organizer. Clear up any obvious or latent confusion about these concepts (see earlier suggestions pages 71, 72) and then give your student six felt-tip pens in six different colors. He should tape one of the concept words on each pen in the following order:

who = green
what = red
when = purple
where = blue
why = black
how = orange

Next, tell him a short story. He must then write the name of the main character in green, write a phrase about what happened in red, and so on following the color pattern. Having done that successfully, he will be ready to read a selection and underline the six elements in their representative colors. Then comes the fun. Ask him to arrange the six colored pens in whatever order appeals to him (point out that it's usually easiest to start with who) and recite a story. As he uses each element in his narrative, he moves the corresponding pen to the other side of the desk. When all the pens have traveled from left to right, he's ready to try it on paper. A hint: Let him write his first draft on index cards. They will allow him extra space for elaboration, and he will be able to physically rearrange the elements until they make a story pleasing to both his ear and his eye.

Second, introduce him to this beautifully simple, easy to remember, and highly accurate organization tool.* Writing is geometrically categorized into these forms:

A newspaper story, which starts with a fact or opinion at its apex and adds more and more supportive material, fits this shape:

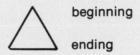

A riddle or a mystery story does the opposite. It starts with a mass of facts and details and whittles down to whodunit.

A recipe or set of directions is simply a consecutive series.

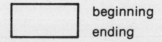

History and literature are either hourglass or diamond shaped. Some, like T.S. Eliot's poetry, begin with many facts, narrow at the middle, and expand again.

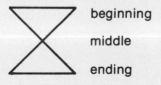

*The brainchild of Aylett Cox, Director of the Dean Memorial Learning Center in Dallas, Texas.

Others, like George Eliot's prose masterpieces, and other well-constructed novels, start on the point, expand, and return.

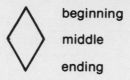

beginning

middle

ending

Draw these forms on an index card for a concrete visual aid to help the student recognize shape and design in what may have previously seemed an amorphous blob. Let him use this system first to categorize what he hears, then what he reads, then what he speaks, and finally what he writes.

The Distended Writer. Some people use verbal bloat trying to appear intelligent or impressive. Generally, young writers between first and eleventh grades don't know how to try this trick and seasoned writers have outgrown it, but the group in between is tempted and often succumbs. This middle group includes those of us who write memos, thank-you letters, descriptions, explanations, term papers, and report cards. Among us, too, are those who teach writing as well as practice it. To do our job well, we must lash ourselves to the mast of restraint and not be seduced by the Sirens of Syntax.

Here is an example of a bloated thank-you letter and its leaner, equally appreciative counterpart, written as samples by the banker who graduated from the writing program described in the introduction. He commented that he found it hard to change his ways since expansive writing had earned him high marks in college.

"Dear Mr. and Mrs. Vail,

I have a fairly strong feeling that a delightful evening had been exerienced not only by me alone, but by all of us who were on hand at your house in Bedford last Saturday night. As a result of some gentle persuasion marked by little resistance on my part what was to have been a very quick stopover for firewood, pleasantly turned out to be a much longer get together than I was originally made to believe would be the case, but every minute of which could not have been more enjoyable.

What made it difficult to turn down your invitation was that it was an occasion for me to savor a delicious home cooked meal which is obviously a rare treat for me these days in which I seldom seem to have the opportunity to indulge. This is due to the fact that life in the city does not lend itself to the same sort of gastronomical tendencies, even in my own kitchen, nor are the environmental qualities the same around my dinner table. A great deal of memories came to mind of the very same spirit in my own family's dining room as I experienced at your place, when I would bring friends of mine home to have a meal.

I found our discussion of the problems that this country seems to be confronted with and our analysis of the direction it might have to take in the future to come to grips with these difficulties to be quite enlightening. It is my thinking that the President's speech last Monday night was unprovocative, and thus ineffectual, and it certainly did not make much of a contribution to my overall sense of confidence in the President's own leadership abilities.

I am hoping that Polly will be burning up her firewood in an expeditious fashion in order that she might avail herself of my hauling services soon again, and thus I might be able to have a chance to enjoy an encore.

Allow me to thank you once again for what was a wonderful evening.

Sincerely yours,

Charley

Dear Mr. and Mrs. Vail,

What a delightful evening we had together. I expected to stay just long enough to gather firewood; however you easily persuaded me to prolong my visit. Your dinner invitation was irresistible. I always enjoy a good home cooked meal, and you made me feel right at home.

Our discussion of contemporary political issues was enlightening. I, too, was unmoved by the President's speech and my confidence in his leadership continues to wane.

I hope Polly quickly exhausts her supply of firewood and requests my hauling services so I may enjoy an encore.

Again, many thanks,

Sincerely,

Charley

For those who would teach writing here are two reference books, three admonitions, and one poem.

Two books: *On Writing Well*, by William Zinsser. Harper & Row, 1976

The Elements of Style, by William Strunk, Jr. and E.B. White. The Macmillan Co., 1959

Three admonitions: Simplify. Do not use two words if one suffices.
Use the active instead of passive voice.
Verbs propel ideas. Adjectives create pauses. Choose accordingly.

One Poem: The written word
Should be clean as a bone
Clear as light
Firm as stone.
Two words are not
As good as one.*

*This is an anonymous poem which Madeleine L'Engle cites in *A Circle of Quiet*.

7.

BUILD A BANNISTER:
Frameworks for Speaking, Prose, and Poetry

Bannisters provide patterns, methods, and formulas which show the student where to begin, and they give him something to hang on to. Far from inhibiting creativity, these supports allow the student to structure and ornament it. Teachers sometimes use the term restrictive expression for such exercises but I prefer the term bannisters because it evokes ascent rather than enclosure. Begin with oral expression. Here are six activities:

BANNISTERS FOR ORAL EXPRESSION

DRAMA

Purpose: absorbing language, empathizing, and developing a sense of audience

Level: * ** ***

Number of Participants: small groups, 2 teams, or a whole class

Materials Required: 1. for pantomime, one situation slip per participant (see suggestions below)
2. for a narrated play, a story, one ping pong paddle or mask per participant (see below)
3. for a costumed production, the works!

Time Required: 1. for pantomime 30 minutes

    2. for a narrated play, 30-minute sessions
    3. for a full-scale production, varies
       according to the selection and the time
       available for rehearsal

Description: Since expressive language begins with gesture and moves through the six levels mentioned earlier, drama is an ideal vehicle for practicing all six. It provides osmosis of language for the student and diagnosis of language development on the part of the teacher. The osmosis comes as the actor memorizes his lines, absorbing polished, cadenced speech. The diagnosis comes because a student will be unable to deliver from memory a linguistic construction which exceeds his own level of language development. Thus, errors can alert a teacher or coach to where a student's language is weak or underdeveloped.

Pretending is often mistakenly considered too babyish for older children, but actually it is an ideal preliminary to higher level academic work since it rests on the ability to abstract, to hypothesize and express "if . . . . . then." The successful actor must understand and immerse himself in another person's point of view, abandon his own persuasions, assume those of his character, and then convey the appropriate emotions to his audience. Seen in this light, pretending is an arrow shot from the bow of abstraction.

Begin with pantomime. Give each participant a slip of paper describing an action or series of actions to act out for the group. How quickly can they tell what he is doing, and how many details do they notice? Here are some suggestions:

    sew a button on a bulky overcoat
    carrying a shopping bag and umbrella and wearing a
       coat, hat, and gloves, make a call from a telephone
       booth
    assemble and mix the ingredients for a cake, put it in
       the oven to bake
    hurry from a peaceful rest in a warm tub to answer the
       telephone

get in your car, back out of the driveway, go down
your street, enter the superhighway, and pay a toll
at the exact change booth

dismantle your beach umbrella, fold your towel, pick
up your tote bag, walk to the vendor, buy an ice
cream cone, and eat it

on the dock pick a spot, arrange your fishing gear,
bait your hook, and cast

on your way to your seat in class with a group of
friends and an armload of books, take a drink from
the water fountain and sharpen your pencil

put on your ski boots, skis, and mittens, and with your
poles get into the lift line

teach a nervous child how to swim, encouraging him
to put his face in the water, blow bubbles, kick, and
paddle

In order to be successful the mime must exercise
his imagination as well as his acting skills. Navigating
around objects which are not there requires the actor to
visualize them and remember where they are. If he puts
an imaginary coat down on an invisible table in the
opening moments of a button-sewing routine, he must
remember where the table is and not walk through it on
his way to pick up the pretend thread. Brainstorm with
your students for more situations to pantomime.

If you and your students want to act out a whole
story but haven't the time to memorize lines and
rehearse a full play, try a narrated play. Select a familiar
story to read aloud. A fairy tale works well. The teacher
should read it through several times to the group and
then select students to play the various parts, including
that of narrator. To avoid the time and expense involved
in costumes, see that each actor has a ping pong
paddle and a small paper bag which will fit over the
head of the paddle. Ask each player to draw his
character's face directly on the paper bag, one side
looking happy and the other looking worried, angry, or
sad—whatever matches the story. The paddle becomes
the character's mask which the student holds beside
his face. An actor is often happier holding a mask

beside his face than he is wearing one over his head, and since the visibility is better, people are less apt to collide. Also a two-sided paddle allows for contrasting facial expressions. The actor can flip back and forth to match the story.

When the masks are ready the narrator reads the story aloud and the cast performs the actions. Everyone participates and no one has to speak from memory.

If your group is ready for the polished performance of a full-scale production, the first step is to choose a script. If you and your students would like to dramatize a favorite story, consult the description of *Playwriting* in *Chapter 8, Stimulate and Stand Back* for a plan of attack. If you would prefer a prepared script here are three sources:

Plays: The Drama Magazine for Young People, available by subscription. For information write to them at 8 Arlington St., Boston, Ma. 02166. The magazine is available for middle and lower school or junior and senior high.

Drama Integrates Basic Skills: Lesson Plans for the Learning Disabled, by Behr, Snyder and Clopton is available by mail from Charles C. Thomas, Publisher. 301–327 East Lawrence Ave., Springfield, Illinois 62717

MEMORIZING POETRY

Purpose: absorbing and delivering beautiful language
Level: * ** ***
Number of Participants: unlimited
Materials Required: posterboard with a drawing of a tree, beach, garden, or night sky; one piece of paper per student in the shape of a leaf, shell, flower, or star; have handy an anthology of poetry or some dittoed poems you have chosen for your students to memorize

Time Required: anywhere from 3 to 5 sessions of roughly 15 minutes apiece

Description: This neglected art and source of enjoyment provides a way for students to absorb and express beautiful language. The teacher provides the bannister—the poem to be memorized—and the student adorns it with his own delivery. The phrase "I know it by heart" is an accurate description of something which has been completely internalized. The poem a student knows by heart belongs to him forever. A little child will chant it, an older student will show off with it, and an adult who must wait in line, endure labor pains, or survive a time of fear may find comfort in repeating it.

Here is a way to set this up as activity for a family, a classroom, or a whole school. On the posterboard, draw a picture of a tree, a beach, a garden, or a night sky. Depending on your choice, cut out enough leaves, shells, flowers, or stars to have one for each participant. When a student has memorized his poem and can recite it, he writes his name on the leaf (or whatever) and tacks it to the tree. The object is to have a tree abloom in leaves, a beach filled with shells, a flower-filled garden, or a starlit night sky.

People memorize in many different ways. If someone already knows how to do it, don't interfere. If he needs help, consider the following suggestions and let each student choose the method which works best for him.

A visual method. Give your student a marker and ask him to cover all but the first two lines. He should look at them saying the words aloud, then close his eyes and say them aloud again. When those two lines are secure he should go to the next two, but in practicing he should always start back at the beginning. That way he will keep attaching additional lines to the body of the poem instead of just accumulating two-line segments.

An auditory method. Ask the student to record the poem on tape, speaking slowly. Then ask him to listen to, and repeat, two-line pieces. As mentioned before, he should start each practice at the beginning of the poem, adding increments as he goes along.

A multi-sensory method. Ask the student to copy the poem in his own handwriting, saying the words aloud as he writes them. Write-say-repeat short segments—a couplet or a stanza at a time. Do not go on to the next section until the first one is secure. If you are using this method with a first or second grader, write the poem out for him in handwriting the size of the letters he makes spontaneously. Ask him to trace over the words you have written for him. In this way he will be able to concentrate on the sight and sound of the words instead of the mechanics of handwriting. The ability to memorize is a valuable skill, and by trying the three different methods described here both student and teacher will learn something about the individual's learning style that will be applicable to other memorizing requirements. Here are some suggested titles:

Kindergarten "Daffydowndilly," by A.A.Milne
An eight line poem celebrating the return of spring, filled with the vocabulary of color and motion.
1st and 2nd Grades "The Little Turtle," by Vachel Lindsay
A three stanza poem about a turtle and what he catches. The repetitive patterns as well as the rhyme scheme make it easy to memorize.
3rd and 4th Grades "The Garden Year," by Sara Coleridge
There is one couplet for each month of the year, helping children remember the months in order and providing imagery for each.
5th and 6th Grades "Bad Sir Brian Botany," by A.A.Milne
Although this is five stanzas long, the strength of the story line makes it easy to memorize. Children this age relish telling of Sir Brian's rotten ways and

have fun with such phrases as "he blipped them on the head."

7th and 8th Grades "Song of Hate for Eels," by Arthur Guiterman

This four stanza description of eels is built on such adjectives as "slithery," "slimy" and "squirmy." Many students at this level enjoy memorizing a description of something repulsive. This fills the bill!

For beauty try "The Whole Duty of Berkshire Brooks," by Grace H. Conkling

This sixteen line poem has some of the loveliest imagery and description of nature I have ever read. If you are looking for it in an index of first lines it begins "To build the trout a crystal stair."

9th and 10th Grades "I Wandered Lonely As a Cloud," by William Wordsworth

This four stanza classic, like the poem recommended for Kindergarten, celebrates the beauty of spring.

11th and 12th Grades "The Lake Isle of Innisfree," by W.B.Yeats

This three-stanza poem speaks of independence and solitude in the imagery of a small cabin set far from civilization.

If these titles do not appeal to you or if you would like some additional suggestions, your students might enjoy memorizing these verses I wrote for my students about colors. You could assign one color to each of six grades or classes, or you could offer the verses, one per month, to an individual student or a class. At the end of six months those who had memorized each verse would be "Through the Rainbow." If you decide to do it this way draw a rainbow on a poster board. Be sure to draw a pot of gold at the end. As each child memorizes the verse for a particular color, let him put his initials on the band of that color on the poster. Students who memorize all the rainbow color verses may put their names on or in the pot of gold.

THROUGH THE RAINBOW

Red

The light that tells you when to stop
Color of a lollipop
Wagons, mittens, ruby gems,
Firelight, roses on stems,
Holly berries, robin red breast,
Red's the color that I love best.

Orange

Jack O' Lantern, leaves of fall,
Topaz, caution, playground ball.
A fruit or juice to quench my thirst
The light that over evening bursts
When the sun has dipped below
The far horizon, orange glow.

Yellow

Forsythia and daffodil
Sunlight over a window sill
The way that Mozart sounds to me:
Bright-lit warmth and clarity.
Canaries, lemons ripe and tart
Cheer and sunshine to light the heart.

Green

Hemlocks in winter, grass in spring
Grapes, beans, or envy's sting
The Emerald City of Oz's Wizard
Surgical gowns, tropical lizard
The color of growth in the cycle of seasons
The innocence of youthful reasons.

Blue

Sapphires, seas, a summer sky
Or a mood that makes you want to cry
Warm blue eyes in a dear friend's face
Blue is ice or first prize in a race.
Rare as blue moon, or cool and patrician
Blue is a color of contradiction.

Purple
Royal robes for kings and queens,
Amethysts, and passion's dreams
Fabric woven shot with gold
Tales of orb and sceptre told,
Sign of Christian majesty;
Breaking dawn. Anemone.

ADD THE WORDS

Purpose: imagining and telling a story
Level: *   **   ***
Number of Participants: single players or small groups
Materials Required: single pictures cut from magazines, 4-page or 6-page picture booklet made by the teacher or wordless books, avallable commerclally
Time Required: 30 minutes per session, as many sessions as you like since students do not tire of this quickly
Description: Tell your students you are going to pass around a picture. After all participants have looked at it once, pass it around again. As each person holds it he is to descrbe what is actually happening, tell what he thinks might have happened before, and what he thinks will probably happen next. Remind them to include all the *wh* elements.

In choosing your picture avoid those which would evoke standardized responses. A picture of a birthday table with the guest of honor blowing out the candles will elicit predictable ideas. A picture of an after-the-party scene leaves room for the imagination—who was there, was it fun, did everyone have a good time, were there any disappointments, did anything surprising happen? A picture of a room seen through a partly open door, a child seen from behind, a wrapped package, or something broken would give each narrator an opportunity to bring in such emotions as fear, curiosity, happiness, and embarrassment. And when emotions are engaged, responses are forceful. The student whose receptive language has been cultivated will be abe to respond with originality and style.

After your students have practiced with a single picture, make a short booklet of pictures (four or six pages) and see if they can invent a narrative to connect all the illustrations with one another.

If you have access to wordless books, use them. In these short, humorous illustrated stories of children and animals, (or animals acting as humans) a story is told through pictures alone, and the reader must supply the words. Children from preschool through grades three or four love them. So do older students, but they are usually embarrassed to admit it. You can help an older student save face while still enjoying these stories by asking him to tape record his narrative as a treat for a younger child. Even adults can use wordless books to practice expressive skills. A twenty-five-year-old Norwegian woman who was studying English used them regularly. Wordless book in hand, she would try to narrate the story a little differently each time to incorporate new vocabulary. Here are two sample titles of wordless books:

The Midnight Adventures of Kelly, Dot and Esmerelda by John S. Goodall. Atheneum, 1972.
Frog Goes to Dinner by Mercer Mayer. Dial Press, 1974.

TELL TALE

Purpose: telling a story
Level of Difficulty: * ** ***
Number of Participants: small groups, pairs, or a whole class
Materials Required: a cartoon strip from the newspaper or a comic book or blank paper or blank film strips with appropriate felt tip pens or an overhead projector, acetate, and pens

Time Required: a 30-minute session or several weeks (see below)

Description: Take a cartoon from the paper or a comic book. Cover or remove the word bubbles and ask the students to supply the words. Or pair your students and ask one to draw a story in sequence on paper (or a blank film strip) and the other to provide the words. Film strips aren't vital, but many students welcome the change from standard paper and pencil work. If you do not have access to blank film strips but do have an overhead projector, you may want to follow the example of Charlotte Goodhue, a miraculously imaginative first-grade teacher who helps her class produce an annual Thanksgiving assembly with a method that works equally well for any topic. She reads aloud several stories about the early settlers and the first Thanksgiving. Then she asks each child to choose one segment about Pilgrims, Indians, victuals, vicissitudes or anything else of interest. He draws an illustration of his segment on an acetate, and, in the familiar surroundings of the classroom and the reassuring presence of his teacher, he tells his commentary into the tape recorder. The teacher puts the components, verbal and visual, together to form a sensible whole. Then, when the great day of the assembly finally arrives, no one need be nervous. Everyone is free to enjoy the children's pictures, projected onto a screen and accompanied by their words on tape. The children and the teacher are calm and confident, and the audience is delighted.

THE FEELY BAG

Purpose: developing descriptive powers
Level of Difficulty: *   **   ***
Number of Participants: small group or whole class
Materials Required: a bag and a collection of common objects (see below)

Time Required: 10–15 minutes

Description: The same teacher who produces the Thanksgiving assembly was introduced to the Feely Bag in a graduate course on language development and now uses it with her first grade. It is a guessing game that fits many levels of sophistication.

The teacher or student hides a common object in the Feely Bag. "It" puts his hand in the bag, feels the object, and must describe it by its properties, not its function, as the listeners try to guess what it is.

For example, an older student described a cassette as "rectangular, thin, hard, man-made, plastic, having two small holes with cogs, one notched edge, a surface which is alternately smooth and bumpy, lightweight, smaller than the surface of my hand." The first player to identify the object is the next "It".

To help young or inarticulate students get started, show them ten or fifteen household objects (an eggbeater, a grater, a can, a nail clipper, a roll of scotch tape, a box of band-aids) and help them think of some descriptive terms for each one. The next day, select one of the items and put it in the Feely Bag. Choose an "It" and let him give the clues. The first player to identify the object becomes the next "It". This game may be used alone or as a precursor to *Common Object*, in the next section.

AND TO THINK THAT I SAW IT ON MULBERRY STREET

Purpose: playing with hyperbole

Level of Difficulty: ** ***

Number of Participants: small groups or a whole class

Materials Required: list of possible topics (see suggestions below)

Time Required: 10–15 minutes

Description: This activity is named after Dr. Seuss's story of a boy who tells a whopper about what he saw walking home from school. Everyone with an active imagination exaggerates, or would like to from time to time: "there was a ton of candy", "I saw a million people I knew", "That hill was as high as a mountain", "my fish was *that* long!" It is the speaker's and listener's ability to recognize the ludicrous instantly that makes "Mulberry Streeting" acceptable—and lying comtemptible. The child who says "I'm taking eight friends to the baseball game on my birthday" when he knows he's only allowed two is an untrustworthy fibber; what he has said is plausible but untrue. The child who says "the whole world is coming to my birthday" is merely a gregarious dreamer. The world scorns one and loves the other.

Timid exaggeration is dangerous, therefore let your students play with hyperbole. If they have trouble getting started, rehearse some elephantine expressions: gigantic, huge, enormous, immense, mountainous, whole earth, volcano, inferno, scorching, freezing, oceans, tidal waves, forever, never, millions, trillions, zillions, and anything ending in "est" ... craziest, richest, worst, best.

Discuss some sample topics and ask each student to choose one and tell about it in hyperbole. Here are some starters; add others as they occur to you or your students:

I saw a man who was ...
I dreamed I ...
My ideal house would have ...
If the birthday fairy granted my wish, she would ...
Guess what! Last Halloween ...
Although they are invisible, the ghosts I know can ...
Once upon a time there was ...
I received a medal for bravery because ...

BANNISTERS FOR PROSE

COMPILATION

Purpose: practicing simple expression on paper
Level of Difficulty: * ** ***
Number of Participants: unlimited
Materials Required: magazines to cut from, simple art
materials
Time Required: 30–45 minutes per session. The
sophistication of the end product determines the
number of sessions required.
Description: *Compilation* can result in a simple collage, a
scrapbook of pictures, or words and pictures together
in traditional or unusual combinations. For example, a
kindergarten class went on a trip to a nature museum.
On their return each child drew a picture of the trip and
dictated a caption. The teacher acted as scribe, and all
the annotated pictures were stapled together to make a
class memento. It is maybe "Mulberry-Streeting" to say,
but this ideas has been used successfully in millions of
disguises by zillions of teachers.

A more sophisticated compilation was the collage
made by the tenth-grade cast of a student production of
a musical version of *Pinnochio*. Starting with a
caricature of the wooden hero in the center of a
36" × 24" posterboard, the students pasted on a
pastiche of photographs showing costumes, sets, and
cast in various stages of preparation as well as scenes
from their final performance. To these they added
words from their reviews (. . . Glorious! . . . Dazzling! . . .
a Stunner!) made from red letters cut out of magazine
advertisements. The body of the compilation was
framed by a black border made up of the participants'
names written in closely spaced block capital letters.
The result was glorious! dazzling! a stunner!

Asking a student to add a few words to pictures

which have personal meaning for him is a non-threatening way to get him started with written expression. Here, as in many other instances in this book, a principle for teaching writing can be used equally well by a beginner or by those who are ready to produce a highly sophisticated product.

ALLITERATION AND ALPHABETICAL ORDER

Purpose: playing with single labels or initial sounds
Level of Difficulty: * ** ***
Number of Players: one student or a whole group
Materials Required: any open book or a Noah's Ark booklet (see below)
Time Required: 5 minutes for alliteration, 30–45 minutes for alphabetcal order
Description: For *Alliteration*, the student closes his eyes and, using any open book, puts his finger on the page. He must create a story whose words all begin with whatever letter his finger hits. Each student should make his story as long as possible. A first grader produced this travelogue: "Wendy went walking with a wet, white, wiggling worm." Needless to say the illustrations which students make to accompany their alliterative stories add greatly to the humor of the concept.

To play with alphabetical order, give each student a Noah's Ark booklet made of two pieces of paper stapled together. He should write the title on the cover and save room for an illustration. At the top of the inside page write this verse:

As the storm clouds gathered
And the sky grew dark
These animals climbed on
Noah's Ark:

At the end write this verse:

Together they huddled
Safe from the rain
Till the dove came to tell them
It was dry again.*

Ask each student to think of an animal for each
letter of the alphabet. If he is stumped on any particular
letter he may invent a creature to fit the gap. He may
either simply list them by name in his bestiary, or he
may prefer to write a couplet about each one or even a
sentence or phrase. Illustrations are welcome. Add
more pages to the booklet if extra space is needed.

In addition to animals, you could ask your students,
individually or collectively, to invent an alphabetical
order menu with a food for each letter. From
applesauce to zabaglione, by way of parsnips and
prunes, it will be a gustatory gambol—or gamble!

If you prefer action to eating, try to collect a sport
for each letter. Feel free to invent some originals to
go with the more difficult letters. Your list may take you
from the familiar archery to the novel zap or zero.

OPPOSITES

Purpose: playing with comparison through opposites
Level of Difficulty: * ** ***
Number of Participants: unlimited
Materials Required: representative lists of opposites (see
below), *Old Maid* or *Concentration* cards, or simple art
materials
Time Required: 30 minutes per session
Description: Comparison is an excellent tool for linguistic
filing and sorting, and it is easy for even little children to
come up with a list of opposites. Here are some
samples:

    * fat / thin
      hot / cold
      day / night

*These are verses I wrote for students in grades 1–6.

good / bad
wet / dry
boy / girl
fast / slow
love / hate

** sweet / sour
narrow / wide
dangerous / safe
absent / present
cruel / kind
polite / rude
before / after
friend / enemy

*** bulbous / slender
imaginary / actual
concave / convex
moist / arid
courageous / intimidated
flexible / rigid
affluent / indigent
barren / fertile

Use such pairs in *Old Maid* or *Concentration*, or you can ask pairs of students to illustrate opposites with words. Pairs of fourth-grade students worte these "something" sentences out on long strips of paper and made a border for the classroom wall.

Something funny is a clown, something
   Sad is my grandfather in the hospital.
Something colorful is a butterfly,
   Something drab is my old sweater.
Something boring is waiting for my
   Mother to get off the phone, something
   exciting is going to the movies.
Something imaginary are Halloween
   Goblins, but scary noises are real.
Something noisy is a motorcycle
   But knitting is quiet.

Something dry is a sunburn but
A puddle is wetter than a sponge.
Something I enjoy is eating pizza,
But I really detest learning
multiplication tables.
Sometimes I am smart, but also I
Can be goofy.

SENSE AND SEASON

Purpose: describing physical sensations and surroundings
Level of Difficulty: *   **   ***
Number of Participants: unlimited
Materials Required: pencils and paper, lists of the 5 senses
    and 4 seasons.
Time Required: 20–30 minutes per session
Description: Here is an unintimidating way for a writer to
    collect the ingredients for a detailed personal essay or
    booklet. Illustrations would be appropriate and would
    help the writer join imagery to words. Here are three
    ways to proceed.

1. Each student writes five short paragraphs
    describing how he uses each of his five senses,
    one paragraph per sense.
2. Each student writes one descriptive paragraph
    about each of the four seasons.
3. Each student writes a paragraph describing how
    he uses each of his five senses in each of the four
    seasons. (5 × 4 = 20 paragraphs!)

Here are some sample topic sentences to begin the
paragraphs.

These are some of the things I *see* in winter.
Winter *sounds* are quiet.
Fires and soup are two of the things I *smell* in winter.
Fruit cake and candy are two of my favorite winter
    tastes.
Snowballs make my fingers *feel* cold.

COMMON OBJECT

Purpose: describing a common object with simple, comparative, and compound sentences.

Level of Difficulty: ** ***

Number of Participants: unlimited

Materials Required: a common object and a collection of linking expressions as a reference for the students. (See below)

Time Required: 30–45 minutes per session

Description: *Common Object* is to writing what the *Feely Bag* is to speaking, but it requires the student to go beyond simple description of attributes and to use more complicated sentence constructions, to make comparisons, and to state cause and effect. It is an activity for a large or small group in which a common object such as a soccer ball, earring, pencil case, sneaker, or T-shirt is on view. The group lists ten or twenty attributes of the chosen object which the teacher writes on the board. From the list of attributes each student picks two and must think of one more that has not been mentioned already. Then, consulting the reference list of linking expressions as necessary, he moves through the five following levels of difficulty.

a) Each student writes three declarative sentences, each sentence containing one attribute. Example:
   The sneaker is long.
   The sneaker is blue.
   The sneaker is broken in.

b) Using three of the attributes, each student writes one declarative sentence and one comparative sentence using a conjunction. Example:
   The sneaker has twelve eyelets.
   The sneaker is smaller than a wastebasket and could fit inside it.

c) Each student writes a sentence containing two attributes and using the word *because*. Example:
   The sneaker is lightweight and flexible
   because it is made of canvas and rubber.

d) Each student writes one sentence containing three

attributes and beginning with a negative conjunction.
Example:
> Although the sneaker is not beautiful
> it is comfortable, useful, and cool.

e) Each student writes a sentence using a cause and effect
construction and two attributes. Example:
> If you leave that dirty, malodorous sneaker
> on the kitchen table, then my appetite will
> disappear.

Here is a sample reference list of linking expressions compiled at a high school in Mamaroneck, N.Y. It is not definitive, but being brief, well-organized, and varied it may be helpful. Encourage your students to incorporate such phrases and words in their conversation and their writing, and leave room for them to add to the list.

LINKING EXPRESSIONS

To add ideas:

and	in addition	and then	equally important
also	likewise	further	in the same fashion
too	again	furthermore	moreover
besides	nor	as a result	because
			since

To limit or contradict:

but	however	at the same time
yet	although	on the other hand
and yet	nevertheless	on the contrary
still	otherwise	nonetheless

To arrange in time or place:

first	finally	soon	here
second (etc.)	at this point	sooner or later	nearly
next	meanwhile	afterward	opposite to
presently	eventually	at length	adjacent to

To examplify or sum up:

for example	in short	for the most part
for instance	in brief	in any event
in fact	on the whole	in any case
in other words	to sum up	as I have said

AS FUNNY AS A RUBBER CRUTCH

Purpose: playing with simile
Level of Difficulty: ** ***
Number of Participants: unlimited
Materials Required: a common object or a picture, one
    posterboard, slips of paper
Time Required: 30–45 minutes
Description: Pass the object or picture around the group and
    ask each person to volunteer at least one adjective to
    describe it. Write the adjectives on the board and then
    ask each student to select one and turn it into a simile.
    Here Is what happened when some boys in fourth grade
    were asked to look into a kaleidoscope. The adjectives
    they used were "pretty", "colorful", "exploding",
    "cheerful", "happy", "even" (meaning symmetrical).
    These were their similes:

> As pretty as snow of all different colors falling from
>   the sky.
> As colorful as confetti on Happy New Year.
> Exploding like a rocketship made of fire crackers.
> Cheerful as rock candy.
> Happy as a fair.
> Even as a ferris wheel.

    Ask your students to write their similes on index
cards. Have one person draw a picture of the object at
the top of the posterboard, then tape or staple the
similes below the illustration. Keep some blank cards
handy and invite additional contributions.

LIKE A VOLCANO ERUPTING, THE TEACHER SAID "NO."

Purpose: playing with simile
Level of Difficulty: ** ***

Number of Participants: unlimited, although this will be just too difficult for some students (see below)

Materials Required: a list of distinctive events (see below)

Time Required: 30–45 minutes

Description: Elicit from the group a list of distinctive events or actions. Use each one as the heading on a piece of paper. If you, or a student, can draw a small picture to go with it, so much the better. Here are four representative suggestions:

> a volcano erupting
> a forest fire
> a mosquito buzzing in your ear
> a soft bed at the end of a hard day

Ask your students to close their eyes and imagine one of the suggestions, then think of another event which seems parallel. A group of eighth graders produced:

> Like a volcano erupting, the teacher said, "No!"
> Like a forest fire, flu went through my summer camp.
> Like a mosquito buzzing in your ear, my sister says, "Help with the dishes."
> It's like a soft bed at the end of a hard day when you finish your last exam.

Write each suggested simile on the paper bearing the appropriate heading. Can your group mint five for each page?

Caution: the literal student will have trouble making similes and metaphors. He will volunteer, as Otto and Nancy did:

> As pretty as looking at those designs
> Like a soft bed at the end of a hard day, I got sleepy.

Neither child was able to abstract the kernel of the experience and transfer it to a new context. This is an important diagnostic signal. Once alerted to it, like an eagle you will spot the trouble.

BANNISTERS FOR POETRY

WRITING POETRY

Purpose: experimenting with imaginative expression
Level of Difficulty: *   **   ***
Number of Participants: unlimited
Materials Required: samples of 7 different genres (see below)
Time Required: as many 30-minute sessions as possible
Description: Some adults are afraid of poetry. Uneasy with symbolism and mistakenly thinking that only the eloquent can write poems, they are reluctant to try to teach an art they haven't mastered themselves. Here dare seven bannisters:

Haiku

Haiku is a Japanese form of a total of seventeen syllables in three lines, most frequently talking of nature. My favorite came from a seventeen-year-old girl who wrote:

> Oh brave bumble bee
> How much in love thou must be
> To kiss a thistle.

Cinquain

Cinquain. When my colleague's son, Scott Welsch, was nine and already a prolific writer, I asked him to teach me how to make a cinquain. He sent me this recipe and example:

> first line: one word, a title
> second line: two words, what it is to you
> third line: three words, something it does
> fourth line: four words, a feeling about the title
> fifth line: one word, a word that refers to or reminds you of the title.

Example:
Hats
Head   Hiders
Warming Your Head
Giving Comfort, Pleasing People
Caps

Shape Poetry

Shape poetry. Let the arrangement of the words on the paper illustrate the topic. Here is the design which came to my mind one summer day as I sat with our eight-year-old son who was trying to catch his first fish.

JULY

small boy

long line

tall pole

deep water

quick fish

Diamanté

Diamanté makes a poem in the shape of a diamond, shifting emphasis on the middle line so that the top and bottom words are antithetical. Here is a recipe and an example.

noun

adjective   adjective

verb + ing   verb + ing   verb + ing

noun about ↑,   noun about ↑,   noun about ↓,   noun about ↓

verb + ing   verb + ing   verb + ing

adjective   adjective

noun

Shark

savage   ugly

threatening   snarling   loathing

ocean   fins   wings   flowers

gliding   soaring   flying

gentle   delicate

Butterfly*

Follow the Pattern

Pattern Poetry. Here is another kind of pattern:

Line 1. Use a word ending in "ing"
Line 2. Use three words that describe appearance
Line 3. Use three words expressing movement
Line 4. Use three words that describe feelings
Line 5. Use one word to summarize

Example: Skating
White,   crisp,   graceful
Fly,   sway,   dance
timid,   brave,   thrilled
Success!

Encourage your students to invent their own patterns.

*(Written by my colleague, Sheila Swett, and two of her fourth graders, Andrew Connell and Tammy Freund)

Rhyme and Reason

Although there's a freedom in writing non-rhyming poetry, rhyming can provide a bannister. Young children are not as afraid of it as adolescents and adults, particularly if the lines can be of different lengths. Here is what Chace wrote in the fourth grade:

IT'S SNOWING

It's snowing
It's blowing
It's growing
It's coming down. It's filled the backyard. We run outside
We slip and we slide.
We pack the snow
Then we start to throw
I run to my sled
The color is red
I sled and I sled
And my face turns red
I sled through the snow. I blow the wind down
I spin round and round
I couldn't hear a sound
I go down
Then I stop. I fly out of my sled
I go down to my head
In the snow
Oh no!
Where did I go?

Thank You, Kenneth Koch

Kenneth Koch's book *Wishes, Lies and Dreams** is pure gold—a fair appraisal since it turns timid teachers into alchemists and gives stilted students a wealth of expression. Here are two adaptations of his patterns and the poems which resulted.

A first grader, asked to write four wishes about *having, going, being* and *an outlandish pet*, dictated:

*Perennial Library, Harper & Row. 1980

I wish I could have a house in the
    shape of a bottle.
I wish I could fly to Mars
I wish I could be a two headed
    rhinoceros with seven horns
I wish I had a twenty-seven tailed alysauros
    that is green.

A fourth grader was given the following assignment: Write a
Never Poem. It does not need to rhyme. Please have one *never*
sentence for each of the following:

1. Something you would never eat.
2. Something you would never wear.
3. Something you would never buy.
4. Something you would never do.
5. Someplace you would never go.
6. Something you always like to think about.
7. "And I promise you I will never . . . ."
    (Add in whatever you like.)

Please use the letter "p" as frequently as possible.
    He produced:

I would never eat pea soup.
I would never wear purple pink polka-dot pajamas.
I would never buy pickled potato chips.
I would never get a pet that's a people-eater.
I would never go to Acapulco to get pulverized.
I would always like to think about popping
    pop rocks with peanut butter.
And I promise I will *never* put a popsicle in my
    Pop's pajamas.

8.

WORD GAMES AND WORD PATTERNS

With apologies for a pun on an old proverb, familiarity breeds attempt. There is no easier way to become familiar with words than to play with them. Word games are as old as language and come by the thousand in all levels of complexity. Here are twenty-one (with numerous variations) which require and expand:

vocabulary
word-retrieval
categorization
inference
logic

These are the same skills emphasized in the receptive language section. Many of the games offered here are the expressive language counterparts of those in Chapter 4. Some are oral, some require writing, and some combine the two. Since many of these games are universal favorites the rules are subject to regional quirks. Play them as suggested here or be guided by local custom. They are designed to tap imagination, tickle humor, and force precision. All three are qualities which characterize good expression

When the word *game* is used as a noun it is defined as *amusement*, *diversion*, *sport*, or *play*. But it can also be used as an adjective, in which case it is defined as *plucky*, *willing*, *ready*. May you and your students enjoy both meanings.

SAME OR DIFFERENT

Purpose: playing with synonyms and opposites
Level of Difficulty: * ** ***
Number of Participants: students alone, in pairs, or small
   groups
Materials Required: word lists and one same-different card
   per player
Time Required: 5–10 minutes per session
Description: Explain to your students that they are going to
   listen to pairs of words which are either synonyms or
   opposites. You are going to say a pair and the listeners
   must hold up the appropriate side of their same-
   different card, an index card marked as illustrated:

	side 1		**side 2**
(green)	Same Synonym	(red)	Different Antonym

   Each listener receives one point for a correct
answer, no points for an error. Call the words from the
two categories in random order and substitute or add to
the following word lists as fits the occasion.

synonyms	*antonyms*
*	
automobile / car	light / dark
chilly / cool	chilly / warm
fast / quick	fast / slow
correct / right	right / left
bike / two-wheeler	before / after
over / above	over / under
**	
damp / moist	damp / dry
vehicle / conveyance	blonde / brunette
enjoyment / pleasure	absent / present
tasty / flavorful	tasty / bland
tough / difficult	tough / delicate
cozy / welcoming	aloof / friendly

***

malevolent / evil	malevolent / benevolent
ebullient / effervescent	elegant / sleazy
contain / restrict	contain / release
hesitate / delay	hesitant / impulsive
austere / restrained	austere / exuberant
habitation / dwelling	evergreen / deciduous

I SPY

Purpose: playing with inference
Level of Difficulty: *   **   ***
Number of Participants: a small group of 4–6 is ideal
Materials Required: none
Time Required: 5 minutes per session
Description: In this guessing game, the participant chosen to be "It" chooses an object in plain sight and tells the other players nothing more about it than its color: "I spy something yellow." The other players try to identify the object by asking questions which are answerable by yes or no. Example:

> "Is it in this half of the room?" is permissable.
> "What half of the room is it in?" is not.

Players soon learn efficient ways to narrow down the choices, and the first one to guess the object ("Is it the yellow button on Louise's sweater?" "Yes") is the next "It".

This is an excellent activity for the lunch table or for any time a group has to wait. A player who hasn't listened to and remembered the earlier questions and answers won't guess the object. For example, if the question "Is it bigger than the palm of my hand?" was answered "Yes", the object cannot be Louise's button. Thus, successful play depends on listening, remembering, inferring, and reasoning. When your students have become adept at *I Spy*, which allows an unlimited number of questions, progress to Twenty Questions.

TWENTY QUESTIONS

Purpose: playing with inference
Level of Difficulty: ** ***
Number of Participants: small group of 4–6 is ideal
Materials Required: none
Time Required: 10–15 minutes per session
Description: This guessing game is a more difficult extension of *I Spy*. The number of questions is limited to twenty; the object needn't be in the immediate surroundings and can even be invisible or fictional. The North Wind and Dracula would both qualify. However, in selecting his item, "It" should be sure it is something familiar to the group.
Sample session:

    1. Q. Is it fictional?
       A. Yes.
    2. Is it a familiar character?
       Yes
    3. Male?
       No.
    4. Is it from this century?
       Yes.
    5. Is it a person?
       No.
    6. Is it a character from a book?
       Yes.
    7. A heroine?
       Yes.

    The inferences so far indicate that the object is a familiar, fictional, female, current, non-human heroine in a book.

    8. Is she an animal?
       Yes.
    9. Is she humorous?
       Yes.
   10. Is she large?
       No.

11. Does the story involve farm animals?
    Yes.
12. Does she die in the end?
    Yes.
13. Is she Charlotte in *Charlotte's Web*?
    Yes.

Here are some other categories a skillful player will establish: animal/vegetable/mineral, size (is it bigger than a bread box?), and use (Is it generally found indoors?).

SPEAK EASY

Purpose: categorizing and word retrieval
Level of Difficulty: *   **   ***
Number of Participants: 1 or 2 players, or a small group
Materials Required: a list of potential categories (see below)
Time Required: 5–10 minutes per session
Description: This activity is a word-retrieval sprint in which the teacher sets a time limit, names a category, and a player earns one point for each word he produces. Students who are equally proficient may enjoy playing competitively while students who need remedial work usually prefer keeping a private record of their own progress. Start with an easy mark and get tougher as your players improve. Example:

> How many words can you think of in thirty seconds which go with Christmas? Ready, set, go.

Four ten-year-old boys who began with the wide category of foods gradually narrowed down to desserts (pies, meringues, frozen yoghurt, cake, bananas) and then quickly discovered how to keep going by sub-category. One boy produced the following list in sixty seconds: *pastry*: pies, tarts, napoleons, cream puffs, eclairs, cake, cup-cakes, upside-down-cake; *fruit*:

bananas, pears, apples, peaches, grapes, plums, canteloupe, honeydew; *ice cream*: sherbet, Italian ice, Good Humors, Dixie cups, ice-cream sandwiches, popsicles, *snacks*: Ring-Dings, Hostess Pies and Funny Bones.

TEAPOT

Purpose: playing with inference and double meaning

Level of Difficulty: **   ***

Number of Participants: one or two players or a small group if the game is played verbally, a whole class if the responses and questions are written

Materials Required: a list of homonyms and some sentences using them (See below)

Time Required: 5–15 minutes per session, depending on how many Teapots are used (See below)

Description: This is a guessing game in which the caller substitutes the word Teapot for each of a pair of homonyms in two sentences and the listener or listeners must deduce what words have been replaced. For example, the caller might say:

"Will you Teapot me at the corner?"

"Please give me some more Teapot."

The first player to guess "meet" and "meat" either wins a point, becomes the caller for the next round, or both. If a whole class is giving written responses, let each student score his own paper. For a list of homonyms turn back to Homonymble (page 87), or any standard homonym list.

I Teapot you could find some Teapot ones.*

*knew/new

PROFESSIONAL BINGO

Purpose: expanding vocabulary through pairing words.
Level of Difficulty: **   ***
Number of Participants: 4 is ideal
Materials Required: one 9- or 25-square *Bingo* paper per
    player and markers
Time Required: 15–30 minutes to rehearse the vocabulary,
    10–15 minutes per session
Description: Follow the directions for making and playing
    Bingo given in chapter 3. As the caller, you name an
    occupation and the listener puts a marker on the word
    which names the product. For example, if you say
    "sculptor" the listener covers "statue", or reverse the
    process and call the word "statue," requiring the
    listener to find and cover "sculptor." The first player to
    cover a complete row of three or five spaces calls
    "Bingo" and is the winner.

       This game is asterisked for middle and upper level
students because younger children get confused; if
they hear "statue" that's what they look for. You should
rehearse the vocabulary with your students before
starting to play. Here is a sample word list of pairs; add
more as they occur to you and your students:

Occupation/Product

    milliner / hat
    architect / blueprint
    carpenter / cabinet
    author / book
    caller / square dance
    dramatist / play
    surgeon / operation
    sculptor / statue
    composer / music
    photographer / photograph
    teacher / lesson
    lawyer / brief

conductor / concert
orthodontist / straight teeth
astronaut / space voyage
chef / souffle
cryptologist / codes
taxidermist / stuffed animals
seismologist / earthquake measurements
comedian / jokes
cartographer / maps
singer / song
poet / poem

User/Tool

surgeon / scalpel
tailor / shears
artist / paint
accountant / calculator
surveyor / tripod
conductor / baton
potter / wheel
butcher / cleaver
weaver / bobbln
sailor / line

fisherman / net
carpenter / hammer
writer / eraser
diner / fork
gymnast / parallel bars
mechanic / wrench
hockey player / puck
explorer / compass

BABY BINGO

Purpose: expanding vocabulary through pairing words
Level of Difficulty: ** ***
Number of Participants: 4 is ideal

Materials Required: 1 sheet of 9 or 25-grid Bingo paper per player and an appropriate number of space markers.

Time Required: 15–30 minutes to rehearse vocabulary, 10–15 minutes per session

Description: The procedure and format are the same as they are for Professional Bingo, but this game pairs the names of adult animals with those of their young. Here is a sample word list:

swan / cygnet
bear / cub
tiger / cub
lion / cub
deer / fawn

hen / chick
duck / duckling
sheep / lamb
goat / kid

dog / puppy
cat / kitten
horse / colt
cow / calf

pig / piglet
seal / pup
rabbit / bunny
eagle / eaglet

CATEGORY SLAP JACK

Purpose: rapid recognition of categories
Level of Difficulty: ** ***
Number of Participants: dealer and 2 contestants
Materials Required: deck of Slap Jack cards (see below)
Time Required: 15 minutes to review the categories and sort the vocabulary

Description: Cut twenty-six 3×5" index cards in half, making a deck of fifty-two cards. On the cards write the names of seventeen things in each of three categories: animal, vegetable, and mineral. Decide which of the three categories is the *Slap* and include one wild card to make the numbers come out even.

The dealer sits in between the two contestants, whose hands are poised to strike, and flips the cards face up on the table, one by one. When a card is turned up in the *Slap* category, the first player to slap gets it and all the cards in the pile underneath. If he slaps a card in the wrong category he must forfeit the cards he has won. They may be returned to the deck or put in a discard pile, depending on how much time the game is allowed to take. Here is a sample word list; add to it as new ideas occur to you and your players:

Animal	*Vegetable*	*Mineral*
flounder	grass	sand
man	lettuce	diamond
bear	geranium	copper
beast	maple	nickel
fingernail	lilac	coal
wool	gorse	steel
fur	beach plum	iron
hair	celery	polyester
feathers	peanut	gold
scales	kelp	silver
skin	pulp	aluminum
ivory	cotton	tin
snail	silk	bronze
cocoon	leaves	granite
leather	tundra	slate
sinew	twig	mica
heart	fern	phosphorus

You can use the same format for the categories of earth, water and air. Here are some sample word lists:

Earth		Water		Air	
dirt	plateau	sea	bay	breeze	smog
sand	hillock	lake	cove	zephyr	thermal-
grit	hump	stream	harbor	puff	inversion
farm	desert	puddle	fjord	gale	heat wave
ground	tunnel	pond	pool	hurricane	gust
mountain	mine	brook	waterfall	tornado	oxygen
valley	burrow	drop	marsh	wind	fog
hill	cave	rivulet	swamp	odor	flying
meadow		ocean		soaring	wafting

ROLL AIDS

Purpose: playing with categorization, association and
pattern

Level of Difficulty: ** ***

Number of Participants: an unlimited number of small groups
(2–4)

Materials Required: discarded ends of window shades (see
below), adding machine tape, or rolls of shelf paper cut
in 4″ or 5″ widths.

Time Required: 30–45 minutes to create, 5–15 minutes to
guess

Description: A hardware or window shade store will give you
(free) leftover widths of custom-cut window shades. The
width of each dowelled canvas strip can accomodate a
word, and in two to six-foot lengths you will be able to
amass a fairly large collection. If you cannot obtain the
window-shade canvas, use similar lengths of adding
machine tape, or shelf paper.

Ask each team to compile a list of words to show to
another group whose job it is to discover what elements
unite the words on that particular scroll. Such patterns
as alliteration, word trains, pairs of opposites and
synonyms, or words which belong in a wide or narrow
category are fun to compile and can be a challenge to
identify. Here are some examples:

Second graders produced a word train in which each successive word starts with the final letter, not sound, of the previous one:

Indian
no
open
nut
table
egg
glove   etc.

Third-graders produced this alliterative allegory:

my
mother's
muggy
monster
made
mud-pies
(in)
my
mouth
(by)
mistake

One sixth-grader asked the group to detect the category for this ten-word list:

canary
hamster
parakeet
rabbit
fish
gerbil
guinea pig
pony

To the answer "pets", he replied, "Be more specific." "Pets with fur?" "Not with parakeet, canary and fish." "Oh, pets which require enclosures or cages?" "Yes."

Two eighth-grade girls stumped their classmates for hours with:

cold air
warm air
sun
snow
slush
rain
happy
bored
flush
broke

"Opposites?" "Not with slush and rain." Finally, "Give up?" "Yes." "Vacations."

HINKETY PINKETY

Purpose: playing with rhyme, syllabication, and definitions
Level of Difficulty: ** ***
Number of participants: pairs, small groups, or a whole class
Materials Required: imagination, humor, vocabulary, and some index cards.
Time Required: anywhere from 5–30 minutes or 3–5 minutes each day.
Description: This is a guessing game based on rhyming definitions. "It" invents one and announces whether it is a Hink Pink, Hinky Pinky, or Hinkety Pinkety depending on the number of syllables in the paired words. The listeners try to figure out the answer. Examples:

Q. "What is a Hink Pink for a happy boy?"
A. "A glad lad."

Q. "What is a Hinky Pinky for a scared boy?"
A. "A yellow fellow."

Q. "What is a Hinkety Pinkety for an especially good Christmas or Hanukkah?"
A. "A December to remember!"

If participants are playing in pairs one should be the

inventor and the other the guesser. Ask them to write the H-Ps on index cards (question on one side, answer on the other) and pass them around to others in the group.

If you are playing with small groups let one student be "It"; the first person to guess the answer earns one point and becomes the next "It". The player who earns the most points in the allotted time is the winner.

If you are playing with a whole class ask each student to invent a H-P and give it to the caller. The caller calls, or posts, all the questions and the students write their answers. At the end the caller calls the answers, each listener corrects his own or his neighbor's paper, giving one point for each correct answer. If you choose to play competitively, the winner is the player with the highest score. If you would would rather not play competitively, call the answers, let each participant correct his own paper, and emphasize the quality and originality of the contributions more than the accumulation of correct responses.

> Q. What is a Hinky Pinky for someone who devours this kind of activity?
> A. A culture vulture.

SWIFTIES

Purpose: playing with adverbs and puns
Level of Difficulty: ** ***
Number of Participants: pairs, small groups, or a whole class
Materials Required: a list of adverbs to help prime the pump, and some index cards.
Time Required: can range from 1 minute for enjoying a joke, to 45 minutes for inventing some. (see below)
Description: Swifties are adverbial puns, linked to the fictional character Tom Swift, in which a quotation is a play on words of its following verb or adverb. Here are some examples:

> "I'm afraid it's my tire," Don said flatly.

"Be careful with that knife," Norman said sharply.
"I need the scissors," Melissa said pointedly.
"Put it in the toaster," Polly said crisply.
"I am a bull-dozer operator," Angus said flatly.
"You think I'm peculiar?" she queeried.
"This letter is for you," Willa said openly.
"I am triumphant," Lucia said archly.

When trying to get the knack of inventing Swifties, it helps to start with a list of adverbs. It is difficult to fish completed ones out of the air. For example, "quickly" might prompt a quotation about sand, "slowly" about molasses, or "patently" about an invention.

To help the uninitiated get started, put the quotations on one group of index cards and the adverbial phrases on another. Ask the participants to match them up in pairs. Next, elicit five or ten adverbs from the group and collaborate on inventing Swifties to accompany them. Finally, collect some additional adverbs, give one to each person and ask him to make his own Swiftie.

"Once the players get going, there will be no stopping them," the author said haltingly.

DICTIONARY

Purpose: playing with onomatopoeia
Level of Difficulty: **   ***
Number of Participants: 6–8 is ideal
Materials Required: a dictionary, 1 slip of paper and pencil per participant
Time Required: 15 minutes per round
Description: "It" leafs through the dictionary and selects a word he hopes is unfamiliar to the participants. He reads the word aloud. If any player knows the word, another word must be selected. Each participant writes a logical-sounding definition on his slip of paper which he hands to "It". "It" reads the whole collection aloud, including the actual definition which he has added, so

all participants hear all the definitions. Then he reads them again, asking the players to vote for the one they think is real. The definition with the most votes wins, and its author is "It" for the next round.

Sample round: The word *anodyne* was offered to six ninth-graders who defined it as follows:

a headache remedy
a valuable mineral from Venezuela
a system for marking years in a calendar
an unusual marking on a coin
a double turnbuckle, used on spacecraft, made of high density aluminum
a food additive now believed to cause cancer in laboratory mice
a substance that relieves pain (actual definition)

VISUAL-VERBAL JOKES

Purpose: making visual puzzles from familiar phrases
Level of Difficulty: ** ***
Number of Participants: anywhere from 2 to a large class
Materials Required: paper and pencil
Time Required: anywhere from 1–5 minutes for solving a puzzle to 30-minute sessions for inventing them
Description: In visual-verbal jokes, a familiar phrase is expressed by the arrangement of words or letters inside a rectangle. For example, if you can decipher:

$$\boxed{\frac{\text{man}}{\text{board}}}$$

(man overboard)

you are entitled to write:

$$\boxed{\frac{\text{stand}}{\text{I}}}$$

(I understand)

Here follows a flock of visual-verbal jokes which have appealed to certain ages, and some of the originals they have invented in return.

A group of New Year's Eve revellers, a faculty member in the winter term, and a group of teachers at a conference in New York enjoyed and invented these. Can you decipher them?

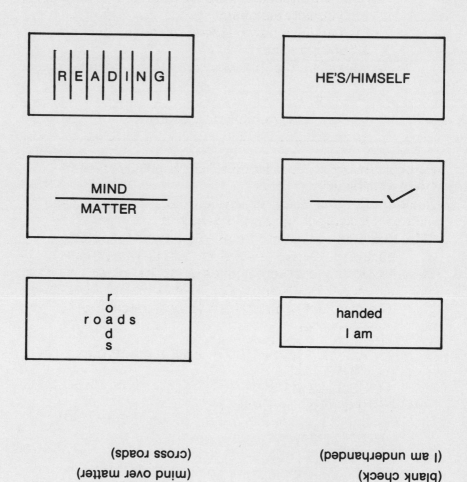

you j u s t me	ECNALG

HAHANDND	FOOT FOOT GRFOOTAVE FOOT FOOT FOOT

PINEAPPLE ƎꓘA⊃	FILEFILE FILEFILE FIMARCHLE FILEFILE FILEFILE

(Just between you and me)
(hand in hand)
(Pineapple Upside Down Cake)

(backward glance)
(one foot in the grave)
(March in single file)

AGGLUTINATION

Purpose: determining origins and inventing new words
Level of Difficulty: **   ***
Number of Participants: small groups or a whole class
Materials Required: 1 posterboard
Time Required: 1–5 minutes per detective session, 5–10
    minutes per inventive session
Description: Agglutination is an amusing, pungent, or
    efficient condensation in which two words are
    telescoped into one word without sacrificing the

meaning of either of the originals. Some gems are consciously created, others are slips of the tongue. Students can play with agglutination either as detectives, trying to figure out components, or as creators minting new words. Keep a posterboard chart of existing agglutinations with their origins, and encourage the creation of new ones. Here are some samples:

Brunch: breakfast and lunch

Smog: smoke and fog

A second-grader, who was watching a counter-man make a delicious ice-cream treat, combined slurp and gurgle when she said, "He just *slurgles* it all together."

A *snurfer* is a winter toy for snow surfing.

A *telethon* is a television marathon.

A new household product for cleaning pots and pans called a *Scrunge* is a combination of a scrubber and a sponge.

When searching for a name for a wit-sharpening word game I combined homonym and nimble to get *Homonymble*. I have always felt that *slash* is a combination of slit and bash and that *gawky* is a blend of gangly and awkward. When the concept of agglutination was first presented to a group of ninth graders they instantly volunteered the examples *cheeseburger* (cheese and hamburger) and *motel* (motor and hotel). Hooked on the idea, they invented *apportment* to describe an important appointment and *surpresent*, a surprise present. They seemed to feel the whole ideas was a surpresent and decided to call the new words they invented from their imaginations *imagiventions*.

ANALOGY BINGO

Purpose: playing with analogy
Level of Difficulty: ** ***
Number of Participants: 4 is ideal
Materials Required: one sheet of 9- or 25-grid Bingo paper per player and an appropriate number of markers
Time Required: 15 minutes per session
Description: Arrange the one word answers to analogy problems in random order on the Bingo grids. The caller reads three-fourths of the analogy and each player marks the missing word. For example, if the caller read hot:cold :: wet: _____, the players would mark *dry*.

The ability to do sophisticated academic work, from mathematics to comparative literature, rests on the ability to think analogously. Practice is productive as well as entertaining. However, remember my earlier caveat: The student who cannot progress beyond concrete thinking into abstraction will be unable to progress beyond simple analogy. The following categories are helpful for inventing analogies at all levels.

Opposites	black:white::rough: _____ (smooth)
Synonyms	slim:slender::fat: _____ (obese)
Rhyme	wing:sing::match: _____ (catch)
Function	gas:car::wind: _____ (sailboat)
Roots	unlock:lock::rewrite: _____ (write)
Object/Agent	farm:farmer::paint: _____ (painter)
Occupation/Tool	farmer:tractor::sky writer: _____ (airplane)

ESSENCE

Purpose: playing with metaphor
Level of Difficulty: ***
Number of Participants: 4 at a time is ideal
Materials Required: the group should be familiar with the

personalities and quirks of assorted famous people
Time Required: 15 minutes preparation time for each famous
person, 15 minutes for each round (times approximate)
Description: *Essence* is a personality-analogy game. Start
with four or five public figures whose personalities and
occupations are very different from one another. Make
a chart or booklet about each one listing such facts as
age, birthplace, career, successes, obstacles, failures,
favorite sports, hobbies, and favorite foods. Be sure to
include some pictures. As the group develops these
profiles they will come to know the people well. Then
play the game this way. One player chooses one of the
five public figures but does not say which one. The
others try to figure out the identity by asking such
questions as, "If he were a color, what color would he
be?" "If he were a plant, what kind of plant would he
be?" The point is not to use colors or plants which the
character owns, but rather those that express the
essence of his personality. One game with ten women
characters and ten children went this way:

Q. If she were a color, what color would she be?
A. An orangey-red.
Q. If she were a snack, what would she be?
A. Watercress sandwiches on very thin whole wheat bread,
vintage champagne, and fresh strawberries.
Q. If she were a book, what kind of book would she be?
A. A slender volume of poetry, bound in blue leather.
Q. If she were a sport, what sport would she be?
A. Badminton.
Q. If she were a body of water, what kind would she be?
A. Fast-moving stream in the mountains with fish and
occasional deep, quiet pools.
A. I know! I know! Katharine Hepburn.

Young children cannot play this game because they
get stuck on possessions. When asked what color best
represents the character, they will give the color of the
dress she is wearing in the picture, or say "blackish"
about every man who wears a suit. But once the group
catches on to extrapolation and symbolism, there is no
end. Continue adding to the central supply of

characters, being sure that each member of the group knows who the possibilities are and has some idea what each is like.

For older children or people who share a common knowledge of characters, the preliminary steps are unnecessary. They are suggested to keep an inexperienced player from choosing his grandmother, whom no one else knows. The children may want to use one another, but before allowing it, the teacher must be sure they will be able to carry it off without hurting anyone's feelings by using accurate but unflattering analogies.*

MADAME MARVELLA THE FORTUNETELLER

Purpose: following directions and playing with rich vocabulary

Level of Difficulty: ** ***

Number of Participants: unlimited

Materials Required: Madame Marvella announcement sheet, 1 My Fortune sheet per participant, 1 die, 1 deck of cards, 2 containers for Personality Fishbowl (and cards for each), Color Scheme chart, Alphabet Board or open book, and list of adjectives (See below for all of the above)

Time Required: 10 minutes for explanation and demonstration, 5–10 minutes for each student to tell his own fortune

Description: Last February I decided we needed something new to chase away the winter boredom, and invented a fortunetelling game which swept through the school. I started with a poster to tempt participants and to explain the components. Since this activity was designed to provide practice in following directions as well as to stretch vocabulary and to enliven mid-winter, I

*My appreciation to Walker & Co. for reprinting this selection from my previous book, *The World of the Gifted Child*, 1979.

made a *Chart of Directions* explaining how to proceed. The students could do this completely on their own. In addition I dittoed a *Fortune Sheet* for each student to use in recording his results. They looked like this:

POSTER

MADAME MARVELLA, THE FORTUNE TELLER

See the Future! Discover the Secrets of Your Personality!

1. Alphabet Clue
2. Nice Dice
3. Pick a Card
4. Personality Fishbowl
5. Color Scheme
6. What's Next

Chart of Directions

1. *Alphabet Clue:*
   If the last letter of your first name is in the first half of the alphabet, consider yourself
   outstanding.
   If it is in the last half of the alphabet, consider yourself *a national treasure.*

2. *Nice Dice.*
   Roll the dice three times. Add the numbers together for your total. The total is the number of your wishes which will come true.

   If your total is an *even* number they will come true *quickly.*
   If it is an *odd* number they will come true *slowly.*

3. *Pick a Card.*
   Cards come in four suits: spades,   , hearts,
   diamonds,   , and clubs,   . Pick a card from the
   deck to learn about your work habits.
   If you draw a *spade*, your work habits are *orderly*.
   If you draw a *heart*, they are *magnificent*.
   If you draw a *diamond*, they are *sparkling*.
   If you draw a *club*, they are *steady*.

4. *Personality Fishbowl.*
   Draw three cards from the bowl. These words
   describe how you usually are.
   Draw one slip from the cup. Since no one is perfect all
   the time it describes how you sometimes are.
   Please replace the slips.

Suggested Word Lists

Fishbowl Words

		Cup Words
independent	generous	disorganized
helpful	musical	caterwauling
witty	unselfish	overwhelming
effervescent	reliable	bull-headed
exhilarating	spontaneous	devious
amiable	team-spirited	ornery
friendly	unique	pugnacious
ebullient	gorgeous	willful
optimistic	spectacular	uncooperative
fabulous	gregarious	bombastic
honest	consistent	stubborn
fair	courteous	balky
courageous	benevolent	reluctant
sunny	remarkable	lazy
delightful	artistic	recalcitrant
fantastic	even-tempered	messy
intelligent	open-minded	noisy
sensational	brave	fresh
marvellous	gentle	outrageous

5. *Color Scheme*
Choose your favorite color and consult the color scheme list to see what it reveals about your energy level.

red	vigorous
orange	high
yellow	consistent
green	variable
blue	unpredictable
purple	highest in the morning
brown	highest at night
black	low until lunch
white	astonishing

6. *What's Next?*
Close your eyes and put your finger on a letter of the alphabet, using the Alphabet Board or any open book. Find the word beginning with that letter to describe your future.

a	assured		n	notable
b	beautiful		o	opulent
c	contented		p	pretty
d	delicious		qu	quickwitted
e	excellent		r	racy
f	fancy		s	stellar
g	gorgeous		t	terrific
h	happy		u	unbelievable
i	inspired		v	venerable
j	jocose		w	wonderful
k	keen		x	(e)xciting
l	lovely		y	yummy
m	momentous		z	zippy

Congratulations!

Put the Chart of Directions where everyone can see it, and spread out the necessary props (the die, the cards, the Personality Fishbowl containers, the Color Scheme chart, and the Alphabet Board or open book. Give each participant his own Fortune Sheet to fill out, keep, and compare.

FORTUNE SHEET

Name: _____   Date: _____

1. Alphabet Clue tells me I am _____.

2. Nice Dice tells me _____ wishes will come true quickly slowly.

3. Pick a Card tells me my work habits are _____

4. Personality Fishbowl tells me I am usually _____,

   _____, and _____, but sometimes I

   am _____.

5. Color Scheme tells me my energy level is _____

6. What's Next tells me my future looks _____.

HOORAY!

UNICORNS

Purpose: collecting and playing with weird, wild words
Level of Difficulty: ***
Number of Participants: small groups or a whole class
Materials Required: posterboard for chart and cards for
   Concentration or Old Maid or Bingo paper and markers.
Time Required: anywhere from 30 minutes to a whole unit.
Description: "Zounds, I was never so bethumped with words,"
   from Shakespear's King John, is a fitting fanfare to
   usher in the Unicorns, a collection of weird, wild
   wonderful words and phrases to collect, play with,
   share, and pilfer. A good one, well-used, will have "the
   impact of a short, sharp anchovy hidden in a strawberry
   ice." (Pilfered from the British writer, Harold Nicolson,
   by C. Northcote Parkinson, originator of Parkinson's
   law.)

Keep your collection of Unicorns on a display chart and let your group become familiar with them by pairing words and definitions in games of *Concentration*, *Old Maid*, or *Bingo*. Here are some personal favorites of mine which may remind you of others. They are words I have met over the years and put in my pocket. Like a comb, a chapstick, a dime, or a Kleenex, they're part of what I carry around. When I need one, nothing else will quite do.

serendipity
cockamamie
chutzpah
hubris
amanuensis
gnomic
iatrogenic
narcolepsy
ergometric
passe-partout
runcible
limerence*
sans pudeur*
interrabang*
anhedonia*

Here are three phrases:

ontogeny recapitulates phylogeny
Occam's razor
to the winds, march

Where would I look to find more Unicorns? Here are six wellsprings:

---

*These four words do not appear in standard English dictionaries. I define them thus:
  limerence: the act or feeling of falling in love
  sans pudeur: shameless, shamelessly
  interrabang: punctuation mark combining a question mark with an exclamation point
  anhedonia: (coined by Woody Allen) the absence of pleasure

The lyrics of Gilbert and Sullivan, whose Mikado gave
me *snickersnee*
Anything by Dr. Seuss, who gave me *hinklehorners*
Brewer's Dictionary of Phrase and Fable, which gave
me *braggadocio*
Bernstein's Reverse Dictionary, which gave me *foozle*
*New York Times Everyday Reader's Dictionary of
Misunderstood, Mispronounced, and Misused
Words*, which shed light on *fugacious* and *pelagic*
*Mrs. Byrne's Dictionary of Unusual, Obscure, and
Preposterous Words*, where I first met *hircine**

Such words are fun to hear and read in moderation, but
the writer must use them sparingly. If every dish of
sherbet contained an anchovy, people might simply
switch to papayas. Used by skillful hands they have
delighted listeners and readers. The anchovy or the
final chord in Haydn's Surprise Symphony give a short
sharp shock. Dr. Seuss's neologisms give rhythm and
an illusion of reality to mythical creatures. In their day,
William S. Gilbert's words delivered a crack across the
shinbone of society.

BOTTICELLI

Purpose: playing with inference and information
Level of Difficulty: ***
Number of Participants: 4 at a time is ideal
Materials Required: general knowledge
Time Required: 30 minutes per session

*Brewer's Dictionary of Phrase and Fable. Harper & Row,
1959.
Bernstein's Reverse Dictionary. Times Books, 1975.
*New York Times Everyday Reader's Dictionary of
Misunderstood, Mispronounced and Misused Words.*
Quadrangle, New York Times Book Co., 1972.
*Mrs. Byrne's Dictionary of Unusual, Obscure and
Preposterous Words.* University Books, Inc., 1974.

Description: *Botticelli* is an associative guessing game appropriate for players who share a common cultural knowledge. In general I have found that while this game angers children younger than seventh grade, it is apt to cause an epidemic in high school. The person who is "it" chooses a character, real or fictional, living or dead, and tells the other players the first letter of the character's last name. Other players try to guess the identity of the character by asking indirect identity questions of "it" which he must answer by furnishing the name of still another character with the same initial. Thus, if "it" chooses to be Romeo he would simply say R. Play might proceed thus:

> Q. Are you a Russian composer?
> A. No, I am not Rachmaninoff.
> Q. Are you a baseball player?
> A. No, I am not Babe Ruth.
> Q. Are you a cowboy?

The questioner must have a specific person in mind before asking his question. In other words he himself must know a cowboy whose last name begins with R. If "it" is stumped by the last question and is unable to come up with Roy Rogers he must give a direct answer to a factual question such as "Are you male or female?" To make the game harder the direct questions can be limited to yes or no questions. To make it more elastic, allow such questions as "Where do you live?" If "it" thinks his interrogator is bluffing and does not, for instance, know a cowboy whose name begins with R he may challenge. He receives one immunity from a direct question for each successful challenge, and must answer one direct question for each unsuccessful challenge. The game ends when Romeo is discovered and the player who discovered the truth is the next "it."*

*My appreciation to Walker & Co. for reprinting this selection from my previous book, *The World of the Gifted Child*, 1979.

9.

STIMULATE AND STAND BACK: Models and Experiments for Factual, Persuasive, and Aesthetic Expression

Through listening and reading we are constantly exposed to three kinds of language: factual, persuasive, and aesthetic. Recognition of these distinctions and familiarity with the requirements of each can pull aside an intimidating curtain of mystery when it comes to trying to write them. The teacher must be sure the student understands which type is expected and exempt him from trying to include all three types in every assignment. It is a relief for many students to be reminded that writing needn't be fancy to be good. The goal should be clarity. Eloquence is a bonus. In addition, writing assignments should be tailored to match the student's developmental level. Fifth graders abhor introspection; tenth graders wallow in it. Plan accordingly. Capture the student's active energy and release his own vigorous vocabulary by giving assignments which make room for humor and a few negatives. Writing—even writing in school—needn't always be solemn and reverent.

The games and activities in this section are designed to provide models and techniques of factual, persuasive, and aesthetic writing and then to provide opportunities for the student to try his own hand. The job of the teacher is to stimulate and stand back.

FACTUAL EXPRESSION

Here are some activities for developing or improving factual work. All students from the lower grades through law school can be comfortable with each.

FOLLOW ME

Purpose: practice in preparing and giving directions
Level of Difficulty: * ** ***
Number of Participants: any number from 2 to a whole class
Materials Required: paper and pencil and a simple prize
Time Required: 10–15 minutes per session
Description: In the games *Airport* and *Treasure Hunt* in
Chapter 2, the student was required to follow verbal
directions in order to come in for a landing or earn a
treasure. After a student has learned to listen to and
carry out spoken instructions, he needs to learn to give
them. This game provides practice in preparing and
giving directions, a more difficult task than students
and teachers may realize.

Imagine that a simple prize, perhaps a candy bar, a
new eraser, or a novelty pencil, is sitting in full view on
the window sill. Choose one person to be the direction-
follower and another to be the direction-giver who must
invent the series of steps which lead to the prize. Tell
him how many steps you want him to include in his
series and ask him to decide whether to give them one
at a time, in sets of two, three, or four, or the whole
series at once. The direction-giver will discover that he
needs to write them down in order to remember them
himself. He and the rest of the group monitor the
accuracy of the direction-follower's performance. If any
member of the group spots an error of omission or
incorrect sequence, he may challenge and become the
direction-follower. Here are some three- five- seven-
and nine-step samples:

Three Steps

1. Scratch your left ear with your right thumb while
   taking three steps forward.
2. Tap your right foot four times.
3. While twiddling your thumbs, approach the prize
   sideways until you can touch it.

Five Steps

1. Walk forward towards the prize touching every other chair.
2. When you are near enough to touch it, stop and click your heels together.
3. Say the first letter of your last name.
4. Cross your ankles and put your hands on top of your head.
5. Jump in place three times and claim the prize.

Seven Steps

1. Get down on all fours and creep to the front of the room.
2. Stand up and say Happy Birthday.
3. Make a 180° turn to the left.
4. Bend over and touch your toes.
5. Skip to the window sill.
6. Say a sentence using the word "delicious."
7. Clap your hands three times and seize the prize with your left hand.

Nine Steps

1. Clasp your hands behind your back.
2. Choose any chair and circle it three and one-half times.
3. Say the color of your dog or a dog you know.
4. Name the fifth letter in the alphabet.
5. Give an even number between nine and seventeen.
6. Walk that number of steps towards the treasure.
7. Say the name of Yankee Doodle's pony.
8. Do three deep knee bends.
9. Walk to the treasure and pick it up with both hands. Remember, they are clasped behind your back.

As mentioned before, teach the listener to visualize what he is going to be doing, pantomime it, repeat it, or jot down notes. The caller, watching for errors in execution, will profit from the same method.

THANKS FOR CALLING

Purpose: practicing taking telephone messages

Level of Difficulty: ** ***

Number of Participants: 2 at a time

Materials Required: pencil and paper and some sample telephone message pads

Time Required: 5–15 minutes per session

Description: Inaccurate telephone messages are usually the result of the listener's being overwhelmed by too much information coming in too quickly. He is asked to sort, write, and remember simultaneously. If, in addition to this, the type of information is unfamiliar, the trouble is compounded, and the likely result is total confusion. The solution lies in providing a filing system into which the listener can slot incoming information. Discuss with your students what they should anticipate:

> who is calling
> for whom
> the purpose of the call
> type of message: will call back, please return call, please tell him the following, or no message

The simple step of predicting probable elements of messages will help the relayer improve his accuracy. Help your students chart these components on forms of their own devising, or bring in a commercially-available telephone message pad. Then ask pairs of students to practice wording, delivering, and relaying clear messages. Teach your message-takers to repeat what they think they heard the message-giver say. This provides a double check on accuracy. Here are some sample topics:

> Your order has arrived.
> Your cousin from out of town called.
> Your mother wants you to do some errands on your way home.
> Elsie is giving a party.

The Yearbook Committee is having a party.

The coach called about the varsity game schedule and some extra practices.

You are supposed to meet some friends at the movies on Saturday.

The coordinator of the Regional High School Committee is trying to reach you.

Your brother called from college about the surprise party for your parents' anniversary.

The classified department of the newspaper called about your ad.

TRAVEL AGENT

Purpose: finding, organizing, and writing factual information
Level of Difficulty: ** ***
Number of Participants: unlimited
Materials Required: some travel brochures or advertisements from the newspaper
Time Required: several 30-minute sessions
Description: Travel arrangements require precision. Collect a bunch of travel brochures or clip some advertisements from the newspaper. Then ask each student to determine the following:

the length, cost, and destination of his trip

the difference in rate for double and single occupancy

the probable temperature

what he will take with him

whether he will be crossing a time zone and, if so, how much difference it will make

the length of time it will take to go from door to door

the relative costs of going by car, train, boat, bus

what the currency will be and how it converts with the dollar

how much money he will take and in what denominations

whether he will take traveler's checks and their cost

how he will get from his house or apartment to the terminal

Ask each student to write a sentence or brief paragraph for each of the above. The information should not come simply in phrases or numbers. (This activity is good preparation for *Take Me Along*, a travel activity in the section on persuasive expression.)

LETTER PERFECT

Purpose: letter-writing practice
Level of Difficulty: ** *** (Even though younger children can and should write thank-you letters, they will not be writing the other kinds discussed here and their thank-you letters can be extremely brief)
Participants: unlimited
Time Required: 30–45 minutes per session
Description: The gentle art of letter-writing is resting in the shadows. Whether it will ever resume its previous role of emotional and philosophical catharsis is hard to say since people are so apt to use the telephone. But probably each of us in the course of our lives will need to write a letter to request a refund, to apply for a job or ask for an appointment, and to say thank you. (Friendly letters will be outlined in a later section under the heading *Tea for Two*.) Meanwhile here are comments, ingredients, and samples of the three types mentioned above.

The Refund Request

Comments:
A refund request should be impersonal and precise, stating your request and how you hope it will be met.
Ingredients:
Name and address of sender at top of paper
Date
Name and address of addressee

Impersonal salutation
Purpose of letter: what is being returned and why
Details of original purchase
Request for refund and where it should be sent

Sample:

John Smith
243 Hillsdale Ave.
Medfield, N.Y. 40392

Aug. 22, 1980

L.L. Bean
Freeport, Maine 04033

Dear Sirs,
　I am hereby returning one pair of size 9 brown blucher moccasins for a refund. They were ordered by mail on August 10, 1980. They arrived on August 20, but unfortunately they are too small. I am enclosing the original order slip and your packing slip and request that you send a refund check to me at the above address. Thank you.

Yours Truly

John Smith

The Job Application or Request for an Appointment
Comments:
　A business letter should be neat in appearance, get to the point quickly, and contain enough facts to interest the recipient in the writer's qualifications.
Ingredients:
　Name and address of sender
　Date
　Formal salutation
　Statement of fact and purpose

Enclosure of resume or brief description of past experience
> (this allows the applicant to tell a lot about himself in a short space and provide the name of a reference)

Creation of a time lapse which gives the recipient time to read the information

"Foot in the door" through resume and request for an appointment

Formal closing

Sample:

Henry G. Trotter
111 Westchester Avenue
Pleasantville, N.Y. 10693

March 11, 1981

Dear Mr. Hoops,

This letter comes in response to your advertisement in the *Westchester Reader*. I wish to be considered for the job of counselor in your sports program. My previous experience includes playing in Little League baseball, Westchester Soccer League, and our town's hockey team. I have been a volunteer at the Bayview Boys' Club where I helped coach younger kids. Three afternoons a week and during vacations I have delivered groceries for Roland's Market. Mr. Bob Field of the Boys' Club is willing to be contacted as a personal reference. I am going away for three days, but will call your office when I return on Thursday and will hope to set up an appointment with you.

Yours Truly,
Henry G. Trotter

The Thank-You Letter
Comments:
   This can be much more informal and chatty. It's easy
to say thank you for a present that hits the spot. Even
if the item is awful, thanks are due. Tact is the writer's
ally.
Ingredients:
   Date
   Salutation
   Thanks
   Mention of the item by name and comments on its
      distinguishing features
   Appreciation of generous thought
   Paragraph of news
   Reprise of appreciation
Samples:

Oct. 8, 1980

Dear Uncle Reg,
   Thank you very much for the soccer ball you gave
me for my birthday. I really wanted one, and this is
just the right kind. You were great to get it for me. I'm
tempted to use it on the driveway, but I know that's
bad for the leather so I'll try to resist.
   Our team is doing better this year. Lots of us went
to summer practice and that helped. Also we're bigger
this year, but so are the other guys so that's a trade-
off.
   Thanks again for the ball. If you ever want to come
to a game let me know. Say hello to Paul.

Sincerely,
Angus

Oct. 8, 1980

Dear Aunt Maude and Uncle Albert,
   Thank you for the necktie you sent me for my
birthday. This is the first one I've ever seen with slang

words written all over it, and with all those colors I can wear it with any pants or jacket.

Our soccer team is doing better this year. Lots of us went to summer practice and that helped. Also we're bigger this year, but so are the other guys so that's a trade-off.

Thanks again for remembering my birthday.

Sincerely,
Angus

CULTURAL JOURNALISM

Purpose: collecting and presenting data
Level of Difficulty: ** ***
Number of Participants: pairs or small groups in unlimited numbers
Materials Required: pencils and paper, cameras, paints, sketch books, tape recorders if they are available
Time Required: anywhere from 2 or 3 30-minute sessions to a whole semester
Description: Through cultural journalism students can increase their knowledge of their own communities and present the facts they have accumulated in original and informative ways. Two admirable, commercially available examples of this genre are *Foxfire* and *The Salt Book.** The first, *Foxfire* (which has since been followed by *Foxfire* 2–6), was produced by students in Appalachian Georgia in 1967. It is impressive for the vigorous enthusiasm it transmits from its creators to its readers. Setting textbooks aside, the students who compiled it fanned out into their own countryside, collecting, compiling, and categorizing information about their neighbors, neighborhoods, and local mores. They assembled their findings in an appealing and instructive product which set the example for the subsequent volumes.

Following in *Foxfire*'s footsteps, a group of students

in New England researched Yankee traditions, customs and lore to produce *The Salt Book* which was followed by *Salt 2*.*

As teachers and students you will enjoy these books for their content and as models, but don't let the magnitude and professional quality of their final product deter you from trying similar exercises on a less ambitious scale.

Through cultural journalism students can give free rein to their natural curiosity, discovering and describing *local history*, *living history*, and *current events* in the school and community. This activity fulfills its promises best when it taps into the students' own interests. They should be encouraged to select their own topics, and their tools should not be restricted to pencil and paper; sketch books, cameras, tape recorders for environmental sounds, as well as human voices, all have a place. Buildings, sagas, folklore, and citizens' reactions to events around them are all appropriate topics. Finally, it is vital that there be a written product at the end of the research which will pull together the various facts, making them accessible to others. Here are some topics and suggestions on how to approach them.

Local History

Brainstorm with your students to make a list of local landmarks. It might include such buildings as the elementary school, the high school, the fire house, the library, the post office, the court house, a church, a cemetery, a monument, the town hall, a corporate headquarters, or industrial plant. If your neighborhood has an outstanding piece of architecture, include it in the list. Also, if there is a local Historical Society get in touch. Their people may suggest places which would otherwise be overlooked. Furthermore, don't feel you

*Foxfire, Foxfire 2, Foxfire 3, Foxfire 4, Foxfire 5, Foxfire 6, The Salt Book, and Salt 2 are published by Doubleday and Co., New York.

have to go way back in history. To someone who is fifteen a twenty-five-year-old building may hold historical interest.

After you and your students have listed some places of interest, consider which ones have kept careful records and how accessible such records might be. For example, a student may have trouble getting hold of the history of a building if it has changed hands frequently or been used for many different purposes over the years. The history of public buildings is easier to find and the people who run them generally welcome student interest.

When the list is ready, ask pairs or small groups of students to choose the landmark they find the most interesting and then see what they can discover about it.

When was it built?
What has it been used for?
How have the uses changed over the years?
Is there someone who has lived there or worked there who would be willing to be interviewed?
Are there any photographs of how it looked in the past?

Other questions will come to mind as they think about a specific site.

See what three eighth-grade students did. In their New England village, the library is a white frame building close to the village green. Through researching documents in the library, interviewing the librarian and a member of the community who had served on the library board for many years, they discovered the following things. Built in 1810, the building was originally the home of a prominent local family with four daughters who never married. On the death of Lavinia, the last daughter, the house became the site of the New England Academy. It remained a school until 1925 when the enrollment became too big for it. The building was bought by the town and converted to a library. Electricity was installed, but there was no plumbing until 1938. The librarian was given an apartment up-stairs in addition to her stipend. After her retirement she continud to live there and was delighted to grant an interview to the team of students.

To complete their project they compiled a thirty-page booklet with a drawing of the library on the cover done by one of the three. The booklet contained a reproduction of the deed, a rubbing of the date on the cornerstone, a written history of the building, a written transcription of the taped interview with the librarian, and a photograph of the students and the librarian in front of the building. This booklet became part of the classroom exhibit on local history, and the creators presented it to the library at the end of the school year. In fact, the final page was a picture and brief story from the local newspaper describing the project and showing the students presenting the booklet to the librarian and a member of the library board.

Living History

Senior citizens have rich and varied stories to tell, and many are delighted to share their recollections with young people. If you and your students are interested in collecting living history you might follow this example as a way of getting started.

A tenth-grade teacher and her twenty-two students decided they wanted to hear some first-hand accounts of childhood experiences in the years before World War I. The teacher suggested they begin by compiling a list of organizations which sponsor Senior Citizen's activities. Through reading the local newspaper they found the Community Center, a branch of the Volunteer Association of America, a branch of the Junior League, a chapter of an association of University Graduates, and several churches.

Together the teacher and students drafted a letter to send to these organizations which read:

"Our tenth-grade class is interested in the subject of

childhood. We are writing to ask if any members of your group have memories of childhood experiences before World War I which they would be willing to share with us. We would like to hear recollections of such things as houses, customs, and holidays. We are interested in how people managed their marketing, cooking, laundry, and communication in times when there were no cars, no microwave ovens, no automatic clothes washers and dryers, and no telephone and television. We would welcome visitors to our class to talk to us. We would welcome letters from people who would rather write than visit, or we could send a small group of students to your center to tape record recollections there. We hope some members of your group will help us collect this living history."

They harvested five visitors to the classroom, two long letters and four interviews which the students taped. Here are some of the things they heard about in vivid detail:

what childhood was like in Lithuania for someone
    born in 1908
childhood winters on a North Dakota farm
childhood as the youngest member of a non-English-
    speaking immigrant family
childhood as the only progeny of a successful father
    in boom times
What it was like to grow up living under one roof with
    several generations

The teacher divided the class into eleven pairs and gave each pair one of the eleven responses to write up first in outlines and then as narratives. The result was a group of living history samples hung on the bulletin board which provided endless amounts of information which the class used for contrasting and comparing experiences.

Current Events

Reporting on current events can happen inside the school or can take students out into the community on field trips. Here are two examples.

The fourth grade in one school made a book about the faculty. All the faculty names were put in a hat. Each student drew one out and was responsible for a page-long report on that person. Each report was to be standardized to include the answers to these questions: What is your favorite thing to do on weekends and why? Who is your favorite author and which of the author's books do you think is the best? What is something you would like to learn how to do and why? What was your favorite subject in school, and how does it relate to what you teach now? Who is the person in history you admire the most and why? Each report was to conclude with a non-standardized paragraph describing the teacher in whatever way the reporter thought most vivid.

In another situation, dwindling enrollment forced the closing of a neighborhood school. In a combined effort, four sixth graders decided to write a book about their school while it was still open. They drew a floor plan, tallied up the number of students, teachers, and staff, figured out how many years the school had served the community, took photographs of the front door and the playground, and included copies of newspaper stories advocating and decrying the decision to close. They concluded with one personal memory of the school from each one of the four writers and a paragraph on possible ways the community could use the empty building.

PERSUASIVE EXPRESSION

"*Persuade*: to cause to do something, esp. by reasoning, urging or inducement; prevail upon. SYN: persuade implies an influencing of a person to an action, belief, etc., by an overt appeal to his reason or emotions; induce suggests a subtler leading of a person to a course of action so that the decision seems finally to come from him; prevail on, interchangeable with either of the preceding, often suggests stronger resistance overcome only after considerable argument."*

Webster's New World Dictionary, Second College Edition copyright © 1980 by Simon & Schuster, Inc.

In the course of daily living each of us is bombarded with all three kinds of persuasive language. Overt appeals are made by those who write or speak editorials ("we urge all concerned citizens to help in the drive to conserve energy"), by politicians ("if you care about fiscal responsibility, vote for me"). From the pulpit and the lectern, from public health officials and merchandizers, from those who promote causes of all kinds come overt appeals urging us to change our ways, cast our votes, buy certain products or contribute money. On the home front parents and children make overt attempts to persuade one another: "Please, Polly, remember not to slam the door." "Please read me that story again, Daddy. I love it!"

Inducement is subtle or subliminal and uses suggestion, metaphor, or repetition. It can be ennobling when we are persuaded to be more generous or altruistic. It can be entertaining. How I wish every January that my husband would capitulate to the inducements of a travel brochure. It can also be irritating or unsettling. I feel resentful of efforts to manipulate my decisions in the supermarket. And adolescents, inherently self-conscious and uncertain of their own charms, are often particularly vulnerable to promises of instant complexion remedies and the high-kissability of washed breath.

Prevailing suggests persuading someone to change his mind. "Oh come on, Mom, you *can't* say no. Everyone in the whole class is going. Please! You've got to say yes."

Students who recognize these distinctions, and have an opportunity to practice various kinds of persuasion reduce their own gullibility while learning a valuable skill. Here are some activities.

PLEASE PUT A PENNY IN THE OLD MAN'S HAT

Purpose: fund raising for a worthy cause
Level of Difficulty: * ** ***
Number of Participants: small groups or a whole class
Materials Required: paper and pencils, simple art materials
Time Required: 3 or 4 30-minute sessions, or a bigger block

of time if you want to plan a fund-raising event in
addition to organizing a campaign

Description: The title of this activity is borrowed from an old
nursery song and is chosen to underscore the fact that
learning how to raise money for a good cause is more
important for students than the actual amount they
collect. Here is an example from our school.

A group of local citizens had gotten together to start
a day care center. They needed equipment badly but
their budget was very small. The head of our lower
school asked each child in grades one to four to help
this neighborhood project by raising money. Each child
was to write a letter home explaining the fund drive and
asking to be given a job which would earn a dollar to
bring in and donate. In their letters the children
emphasized that they were not asking for handouts but
rather opportunities to help younger children. The
children took great pride in their ability to explain, earn,
and contribute.

When a fund drive was begun to expand the
playground and park facilities in one New England
town, a group of high school students wanted to raise
money. They decided to offer their services as baby-
sitters, grass-cutters, errand-runners, cooks, dish-
washers and car-washers, painters, attic-cellar-and-
garage cleaners, and pet watchers. They planned to
give the money they would have earned to the park
fund. This is how they organized their effort.

First they made a poster to hang in the front hall of
the school. It had a picture of the park, a written
explanation of the fund drive, a statement of how
improved park facilities would benefit the town, why
high school students should help the cause, and how to
go about it. Then they posted sign-up sheets asking
students to volunteer $5.00 worth of work in the eleven
categories mentioned, or any other category a student
might suggest. (One volunteered introductory guitar
lessons at $1.00 per half hour.)

One member of the group wrote a letter to the local
newspaper describing the project and asking for free

publicity for the services the students could provide, and explaining how to obtain them. Another member offered to put the volunteers in touch with those requesting workers.

More than three hundred students signed up, netting over $1,500. for the park. Overt persuasion worked well for a good cause.

PROVERBS

Purpose: exploring the language of persuasion
Level of Difficulty: **   ***
Number of Participants: unlimited
Materials Required: a list of proverbs (see suggestions below)
Time Required: as many sessions of 30–45 minutes as you wish
Description: Proverbs are pithy exhortations to desirable behavior. They frequently urge caution, as in the old gambler's saying "trust your Mother, but cut the cards", and they proselytize moral values. Collect a list and post it in plain sight. Here are some samples to start you off:

1. A stitch in time saves nine.
2. Spare the rod and spoil the child.
3. Don't count your chickens until they hatch.
4. Fine words butter no parsnips.
5. Pride goeth before a fall and a haughty spirit before destruction.
6. A fool and his money are soon parted.
7. Two heads are better than one.
8. Don't put all your eggs in one basket.
9. The pen is mightier than the sword.
10. You will catch more flies with honey than with vinegar.
11. Don't cry wolf.

Go over these samples with your class. If you are working with a group of ten students pick ten proverbs, discuss them, and extract the kernal of meaning from each. Then give each student one and ask him to write a story exemplifying the principle without mentioning the maxim. When the story is done the author should read it aloud and ask the class to decide which proverb it matches.

For example, a third-grade girl wrote a parallel to "don't cry wolf." She described a little girl who always said she had a sore throat when it was time to go to school. By lunchtime her throat was always better, and she could go outside in the afternoon to play. One day she said her throat was sore, but her mother didn't believe her and made her go to school. She felt awful all day with itches under her tights and long sleeves. She went to the school nurse to complain, but still nobody believed her until some other children started teasing her about the funny-looking stuff all over her face. That was the day she came down with chicken pox.

There is no mistaking the message of a proverb. Even though it is cast in metaphor it is overt persuasion, with no pretense of subtlety.

BUY BUY BIRDIE

Purpose: experimenting with advertising
Level of Difficulty: ***
Number of Participants: anywhere from 2 students to a whole class
Materials Required: pencils, paper, simple art materials, and a tape recorder if one is handy
Time Required: roughly 5 sessions of 45 minutes each, longer if you wish
Description: This is suitable for two students or a whole class and can be an in-depth, long-term project or it can last a week. Either way, this action-packed, highly entertaining game of overt persuasion and inducement

is particularly popular with students between grades six and twelve. Here are four steps to follow.

Step One

Elicit from the students themselves a list of words and phrases they associate with advertising and persuasion. Ask them to bring in samples from radio, television, magazines, newspapers, and supermarkets. Get them questioning various sales pitches.

If you want to buy something but fear you are being self-indulgent, is your guilt assuaged by the phrase *you owe it to yourself*? Example: "You work hard all day studying. When you are through you owe it to yourself to enjoy the taste of Butter-All Pound Cake."

Does panic feed a sense of inadequacy when you hear or read *without* and *unless*? Example: "Without Season-All your hamburgers will be bland and uninteresting." "Unless you, too, carry a Sensound transistor radio you won't be up to date."

Does the promise of perfection lure you when you meet *you too will*? Example: "With the purchase of these designer jeans you, too, will join the ranks of those who stand out in a crowd."

Step Two

Ask your students to invent a mythical product: a candy bar, cold cereal, anti-dandruff shampoo, or a new kind of board game. Decide on its ingredients, salient features, name, and price. Divide the group into advocates and detractors.

Step Three

Each side concocts the following five things either in favor of or warning against the product: a radio advertisement, a jingle, a slogan, a newspaper advertisement, and an editorial. Encourage your students to use some of the phrases, words, and techniques they explored in *Step One*. Each side should display and broadcast its five elements in whatever way fits the layout of the classroom. The newspaper advertisement, slogan, and editorial can be on a bulletin board, and the jingle and radio advertisement can be on a cassette.

Step Four

When all the elements of the campaign are prepared and assembled, each side presents its case to another class or group, giving each member of the audience a slip of paper saying

Yes, I would buy _____ because (25 words or less)

No, I would not buy _____ because (25 words or less)

Tally up the score and see which side wins.

TAKE ME ALONG

Purpose: analyzing and using the language of advertising
Level of Difficulty: ***
Number of Participants: anywhere from 2 students to a whole class
Materials Required: pencils, paper, simple art materials, sample travel folders, or magazines and newspapers with travel advertisements, and a tape recorder if one is handy
Time Required: roughly 5 sessions of 45 minutes each
Description: Like *Buy, Buy Birdie*, this variation on the advertising campaign theme gives students an opportunity to peruse and practice overt persuasion and inducement. Divide the group into two teams each of which must invent a hypothetical resort: vacation spot A and vacation spot B. They should study a bunch of travel advertisements for samples of ways to make a spot seem irresistable. Then each team plans a three-step campaign to lure potential customers.

Step One

Design a brochure with copy that will provide enticing information about the setting, sports, sight-seeing, accomodations, and cost.

Step Two

Design a 5 × 8" advertisement to run in the local paper.

Step Three

Make up a one-minute commercial to be broadcast on the local radio station.

One campaign tries to persuade people to come to vacation spot A and the other to the rival spa. Present both campaigns to another class or group. Which spot wins the most votes and why did the voters choose as they did?

THERE SHOULD BE A LAW

Purpose: using different techniques to persuade people to your point of view
Level of Difficulty: ***
Number of Participants: anywhere from 2 to a whole class
Materials Required: pencils, paper, and several issues of the local newspaper
Time Required: as many 45-minute sessions as you care to devote
Description: Pick a local issue and plan a campaign to convert people to your point of view. Incorporate each of the following:

1. A slogan
2. A three-minute speech
3. A letter to the editor of the local newspaper
4. A letter to your local radio station requesting air time to present your thoughts
5. A bumper sticker

Here is an example. Last year our school board voted to close one of the five elementary schools because of the decline in the number of elementary school children in the district. When the board voted to close the Bedford Village school, many of the residents were upset and mounted a campaign to try to reverse the decision. The slogan they chose was *S.O.S.* (Save Our School), and the local press and radio gave the situation extensive coverage. Students of many ages, from that school and the other four schools, expressed their opinions using the elements described above. No matter what the outcome (the board did not reverse its decision), being actively involved in a divisive local issue was a learning experience for all. Students and adults drew upon their reservoirs of skill in overt persuasion and inducement in their efforts to prevail.

SHOW OFF

Purpose: an experiment in writing, packaging, marketing, and evaluating

Level of Difficulty: ***

Number of Participants: anywhere from a single student to a whole class

Time Required: 4 or 5 45-minute periods

Materials Required: pencils, paper, and a copy of the outline below

Description: Give each participant a copy of this outline and encourage him to add any elements he thinks would improve it.

Outline

1. There is going to be a new TV program. You are the author and will be paid $5,000 for the script. Make your choices from these lists:

   category
   adventure
   science fiction

family show
comedy
mystery
documentary

Time
the present
colonial days
the year 2076
prehistoric time
other _____

characters (mark the hero with H and the villain
    with V)
animal (what kind?)
soldier
cowboy
doctor
explorer
scientist
farmer
child
other _____

Choose a name for your hero and your villain:
    hero_____
    villain_____

the cause of the conflict is
power
jealousy
dishonesty
money
beliefs
danger
differences in personality

confrontation
physical combat
devious tricks
argument
other _____

outcome
the victor is _____ because _____ was
honest
more loyal
luckier
smarter
trickier
bigger
nobler
braver

name of show
_____

2. Write a newspaper ad for your show which will make the reader really want to see it.
3. An actor or actress you really admire is _____. Write this performer a letter offering the starring role in your show. You should mention the reasons you feel his or her talent particularly matches the requirements of the role, the salary you are willing to pay, when rehearsals will start, where they will take place, and who the other members of the cast will be. You will need to offer good inducements because this performer has a busy schedule!

4. All the people in your school want to see your show but they have a great deal of homework. Write a letter to your principal suggesting that viewing be encouraged (or mandatory, if you are feeling brave) for all students and faculty. Your letter will have to have perfect spelling, good grammar, and excellent reasoning in order to prevail. Good luck!
5. Now you need a sponsor. Decide what audience your show is likely to attract. Then decide what kinds of products this audience is apt to buy. Write a letter to the president of a company that makes such a product and ask him to be the sponsor. Point out the benefits he is apt to reap.
6. Now abandon the role of author and assume the role of critic. Write a review of the first episode.

AESTHETIC EXPRESSION

Students who have been exposed to the earlier exercises in this book, who have soaked up rich vocabulary, rhythm, and cadence, and who have been captured by characterization, narrative, humor, and dialogue through listening and reading are ready to try producing parallel work. Here are some activities which expose the student to models and encourage him to experiment. The student may be asked to reproduce his own version of a model as we will see in *Trolls and Myths*. He may be encouraged to extend a model as we will see in *A Laugh and a Half*. He may practice shifting a story from prose to dialogue as in *Curtain Time* or he may try describing a single event from several different vantage points as we will see in *Tea For Two*. As with the sections on *Factual Expression* and *Persuasive Expression*, the teacher's role is to stimulate and stand back.

TROLLS AND MYTHS

Purpose: creating mythical creatures and myths
Level of Difficulty: * ** ***
Number of Participants: unlimited
Materials Required: a group of stories or book about trolls and a collection of myths
Time Required: as many 30- to 45-minute sessions as you are willing to give
Description: This activity is designed to help your students invent creatures and stories from their own imaginations. Although the products will be original they are also part of literary tradition.

Trolls

Both in literature and in individual imaginations trolls come in all sizes and shapes. They can be benevolent, mischievous, or evil, and since there is no standard recipe for concocting a troll or predicting his adventures, imagination can run free.
Begin by reading a story about trolls or a

description of them to your group. A favorite book of mine is *Trolls**, but there may be another you prefer or you may want to write your own. At any rate, after you have read one or two short selections aloud, discuss with your students what they think those trolls looked like and how they behaved. Then read another selection and ask the students to illustrate what they have heard. Finally, ask each student to invent, describe, illustrate, and name his own troll and then write an adventure for him. This simple-sounding exercise is equally appealing to fourth through twelfth graders.

Myths

Myths offer answers to questions people have asked through the ages—where did the stars come from, why does the moon change shape, what would happen if . . . , what is the reason for seasons, and where do people go after they die? The Greeks, the Norsemen and the Indians, to name but three from a long list, all had different explanations, but there is remarkable similarity in the questions they explored through mythology.

Some myths describe what happened "ever after" in the wake of an event. Others show how an event represents a culmination of forces. After reading five or six myths aloud to your group ask them to write an original one or a reaction to a mythical explanation. Here are some starters and two examples. List 1 offers sample beginnings; List 2 offers sample conclusions. Use them independently of one another, or take the beginning from List 1 and the conclusion from List 2 and ask your students to fill in the middle. By all means encourage your students to invent their own starters.

List 1

Once upon a time, snow fell and fell and didn't know when to stop.

*P. & I. d'Aulaire, *Trolls*. Doubleday & Co., Inc. 1972

In a long ago time, the sun threatened to leave the
earth.
There was a day when music first came to the earth.
Once upon a time, Spring couldn't decide when to
appear.
Once upon a time, Fire grew angry.
Rain had never come to the earth until . . .
Once upon a time the bears decided to stay awake all
year.

List 2

And ever since that time each snowflake has been
unlike any other one, each beautiful, each unique.
And ever since that time the sun disappears for a
certain number of hours but always returns.
And ever since that time there has been music.
And ever since that time Spring has always returned.
And ever since that time, people have made boundaries
for Fire.
And ever since that time rain has been welcomed on the
earth.
And ever since that time bears have hibernated.

After hearing five or six myths about the origins or
natural phenomena, a group of six second graders in
our school brainstormed to invent this myth which they
dictated to their teacher, Sally Thacher.

Second Graders' Myth

One night long, long ago a man looked up in the
sky. It was very dark and he wished for some light so he
could see the path ahead of him. There was a famine in
his village because the hunting was not good during the
day and it was too dark at night to hunt. He prayed for
food for his people. When he reached his village, he and
the other hungry hunters were so angry that they threw
rocks at the sky. But nothing happened.
Suddenly, a huge rumbling was heard as a
mammoth attacked the village, and many people fled in
panic. The men who were throwing rocks at the sky in

anger began hurling them at the mammoth. But it only made him more ferocious. Many of the rocks missed their target because of the darkness; the mammoth was not slowed down at all.

Another rumbling was heard, but this time in the sky. A storm was approaching! It was a violent thunderstorm with heavy rains and much lightning. lightning set fire to the forest. The flames and sparks leaped so high in the sky that the rocks thrown by the hunters caught fire. This gave them enough light to kill the mammoth.

By the time the storm had passed, the people had food in plenty for months. And they had light in the night sky to help their hunting. From then on, those burning rocks were known as stars.

Here is a poem written by a high school student whose class had been reading and discussing the mythology of the rhythm of the seasons and of the underworld. This student was particularly intrigued to discover that during the Dark Ages, in parts of Europe, people ascribed magical powers to bears. Their erect posture made these animals seem nearly human, while their hibernation, during which they appeared dead until they miraculously returned to life in the spring, made them seem superhuman. People used to leave messages for departed souls at the dens of hibernating bears, assuming that these creatures had found a way to visit—and return from—the land of the dead.

The Return of the Bear

With hairy paws
The wakening Bear
Hangs garlands
Of woodland roses
On the walls of the forest
Sprinkling them with water
From the spring-time sea.

Where went you, Bear
In your seeming sleep,
To the sunless kingdom
Under the earth
Where the souls of the dead
Whisper their journeys' events
And wait for others to come?

Welcome, Bear
From your winter's dreaming travels
To sunshine
And shadows of the earth
The morning tang
And the wind that blows
From the South.

A LAUGH AND A HALF

Purpose: playing with humorous poetry
Level of Difficulty: * ** ***
Number of Participants: anywhere from 1 to a whole class
Materials Required: a few samples (see below)
Time Required: as many 30 to 45-minute sessions as you can
arrange
Description: Humorous poetry is magnetic and contagious. If
you are looking for suggestions of authors, here are five
favorites of mine whose verse is well-represented in
standard anthologies:

Edward Lear
Hilaire Belloc
Lewis Carroll
Ogden Nash
Gelett Burgess

If you are looking for variety within the covers of a
volume, here are two excellent sources. *The 1979
Oxford Book of American Light Verse* is a puckish
pastiche offering samples and examples, and *Where*

the Sidewalk Ends, by Shel Silverstein,* a collection describing zany, impossible creatures and happenings, is an excellent springboard to original work.

One group of third graders read Silverstein's poem "Sarah Cynthia Sylvia Stout Would Not Take the Garbage Out," the tale of a stubborn young lady who would not do her chore. Silverstein describes the accumulation of rotting garbage in exquisitely vile detail. After the students had had several chances to savor each gruesome bit, they invented their own verses describing garbage-can contents. We stapled their verses to a drawing of a garbage can labeled "Great Garbage." Here are four samples:

1. Old bananas, mushy tails
   Of fish and shrimp and trout and whales
   Dried up bean cans from the beans
   Rotten ends of submarines.

2. Crushed-up, mushed-up lollipops
   Rusty broken bottle tops
   Purple spotted old band-aids
   Ripped up moppy window shades
   Mystery mushrooms, sour cider
   Kitty litter, squished-up spider.

3. Dried up splintered chicken bones
   Wet old soggy styrofoam
   Ham and eggs from yesterday
   Brings a smell along the way
   With a lot of meat and mush
   And one ton of gooey gush
   As we fill the garbage pail
   It piles up and we turn pale.

4. Dribbling drooling purple egg-nog
   Slimy leg and skin of frog
   Snouty mouty old fish heads
   Cookie crumbs from unmade beds.

Frequently students who are reluctant to try lyrical or emotional poetry are less timid about humor, and

*Harper & Row, 1974.

having laughed over the examples you have provided,
they will delight in trying to produce companion pieces.
Humor can be a dowser's wand to the pools of affect
and energy which are part of real learning. From
limericks can come laughter and from doggerel, delight.

CURTAIN TIME

Purpose: practice in converting prose into dialogue
Level of Difficulty: *   **   ***
Number of Participants: a small group of 4–6 is ideal, or a
    whole class together if necessary
Materials Required: a favorite story, some index cards, and
    pencils
Time Required: varies according to the length of the play (see
    below)
Description: This simple technique for converting prose to
    dialogue works with students of all ages and all levels of
    language development. Even very young children can
    write a play. Choose a story you think the group will
    enjoy, and read it aloud. Fairy tales work very well.
    Encourage your group to discuss the story: how do you
    feel about the characters; which ones do you like; which
    ones can you trust; which ones are sad inside; how do
    people walk, sit, look, talk when they are happy, sad,
    scared or angry; how do you feel about the ending; what
    part of the story is the most suspenseful; what is the
    climate of the setting; what kind of clothing would
    people wear in that climate; and so forth.
        Then assign parts to students randomly and ask the
    characters to pantomime the plot as you re-read the
    story. Re-read it again, this time asking, "What do you
    think he would say when he sees the axe?" "How would
    she describe her feelings?" It won't be long before the
    group agrees on the dialogue, and because it came
    from them they will be able to remember it.
        As the script jells, transcribe the dialogue onto

index cards. If there are two competing versions of an episode, write them both out, read them aloud, and take a vote. When most of the dialogue is set read it through aloud asking the students to listen for any elements of the plot which may be missing: "Oh, we forgot to get the lion in here. How shall we do it?" Index cards can be rearranged, and there's always room to insert a missing piece. Before you know it the script will be finished, written by the students in language which they can use and remember easily because it was theirs to begin with.

A kindred technique is used by Gerald Chapman who headed a playwriting project for students in England. He brought it to this country in 1981 under the title Young Playwrights Festival.* Starting with an imaginary situation such as an eviction scene involving a condemned house, a domestic scene with someone missing from an accustomed place at the kitchen table, or a mysterious scene involving the sudden unexplained sounds of gun-shot, the teacher encourages the students to discuss what they think is happening and what may have preceded the current situation. When there is agreement on the story line, each student is given a short time (perhaps twenty minutes) to write it out in dialogue. Then the students read their versions aloud and share their reactions. Through discussion such as this young playwrights begin to realize how to convey emotion and plot through action as well as dialogue. Finally each student takes a longer period of time (perhaps an hour and half) and rewrites his scene which he again shares with the group. Chapman uses other similar devices from one-word scene starters to brief character sketches to practice the same principle: He cultivates student playwriting through the words students use themselves in discussing situations and stories which engage their emotions.

*contact The Dramatists Guild, 234 West 44 St., New York, N.Y. 10036 for additional information.

TEA FOR TWO

Purpose: practicing letter-writing to develop a sense of
        audience
Level of Difficulty: **   ***
Materials Required: pencils, paper, and a list of events
Time Required: 10 minutes per letter, 3 letters per episode,
        thus 30 minutes per set and extra time for proofreading
Description: Help a student develop and focus his sense of
        audience by asking him to vary his listeners. A sample
        assignment might be:

Something Embarrassing

"It was so embarrassing at the restaurant. After I had
finished my hamburger, dessert, and drink, I realized that
my money was at home." Write three letters describing this
event—the first to a friend, the second to a dignified
grandparent, and the third to a visitor from another planet.

Here are some other categories with a sample situation
for each. The first three situations are complete
episodes. The next five are open-ended, leaving the
writer greater opportunity for originality.

Something Exciting. It was nearly time for the curtain to
go up. We had been rehearsing all month, and the dress
rehearsal had gone badly. That's meant to be lucky, so
we were all feeling optimistic. All of a sudden I couldn't
remember my first line. Before I could tell anyone, the
curtain started up!

Something frightening. We had agreed it was time to go
home. We had been in the abandoned house nearly all
Halloween, but when we got to the door a figure was
blocking it!

Something Embarrassing. I was talking on the
telephone to Charlotte. We were talking about Polly. I
heard a voice say, "Well, is that so?" I looked up and
there was Polly standing in the doorway!

Something Athletic. The tennis coach signed me up to play in the doubles tournament with someone I had never even met. He said he thought we were about equal, and he predicted we would make a good team. This is what happened.

Something Beautiful. The museum is having an exhibit of pictures by a new artist. I had never heard of her or seen her work, but I went and was amazed. This is what it was like.

Something Romantic. I was walking down the hall when I heard someone call my name. I stopped and turned around. For weeks I had been hoping that very person would speak to me, but how could that happen since we had never been introduced? It seemed like a miracle, and guess what happened next?

Something Funny. The puppy ran into my room, and you'll never guess what he had with him when he came out!

Something Heartwarming. I made a new friend today. This person is not at all like my other friends. In fact, this person isn't like anyone I've ever met before. Let me explain.

This sampling is the start of a collection of exercises and explanations which can cover a wide range of human events and emotions. Encourage your students to add to these categories, samples, and types of audience to which the letters are directed.

PART III._____

Proficiency

10.

YEAR IN, YEAR OUT:
A School-Year Calendar
of Writing Activities

Here is a calendar of writing activities for an individual, a small group, a class, a club, a family, or a whole school. Each month's activity could be subdivided infinitely, providing a suggestion for each week or even for each day.

Although the descriptions vary in length from month to month, each activity can be done quickly or in depth depending on the interest and skill of the participants. The activities may serve as extensions, reminders, or refinements of skills acquired earlier, or they may form a skeleton on which to flesh out the language arts curriculum for the year. They are appropriate for students at all levels of sophistication. For the older student who wants a way to practice writing in relative privacy, this calendar provides organization and variety, and for the timid student who fears he cannot produce works of variety or value, here are a painless ways for him to discover his capacity. Very young children may need help with the mechanics of reading or writing, but most of the ideas are not beyond them.

The writer who writes a little bit every day and who always has a project in progress will improve simply through practice. Some work will be for his eyes only. The pieces he wants to polish for public viewing will need pruning, trimming, and shaping. Every good writer rewrites. To return to our earlier metaphor, once cultivation has yielded expressive growth, shaping becomes an exercise in artistic proportion. Pruning, a learnable skill, can be performed on a fat, full hedge but not on a row of leafless spindles. Here are five maxims which may keep rewriting to a minimum:

1. Use the active not the passive voice.
2. Rely on verbs instead of adjectives to move your thoughts along.
3. Shun bloat.
4. Proofread with your ears as well as your eyes. You will hear the difference between a sentence fragment and a sentence before you will see it. Putting commas where you *hear* the need for a pause produces the convivial, "When do we eat, Mom?" instead of the cannibalistic, "When do we eat Mother?"
5. The shape of a paragraph is a visual reminder that this is a group of thoughts which belong together. Let the reader know the topic in the first sentence. Save your punch line for the end.

The asterisk and coding system I have used in previous sections of the book is modified here since each activity can be done independently and all of them are appropriate for all three levels of proficiency.

Being a teacher, I always think of September as being the first month of the new year, so that's where this calendar begins. These are the topics:

September: Labels
October: Beasts
November: If
December: Holidays
January: Description
February: Fairy Tales
March: Poetry
April: Biography
May: Autobiography
June: Journals

SEPTEMBER: LABELS

A skillful writer guides his reader's thoughts without being obviously bossy. The reader's attention is like water. Vague vocabulary encourages it to flow in all directions. Precise words channel it. If given "I saw the thing but it went," the reader is free to imagine a thing of any size, shape, or disposition whose departure could have been a relief, a disappointment, or a matter of no importance. Perhaps *the thing* is a bird. In reading "I saw the bird, but it flew away," the reader is free to imagine a robin redbreast or an albatross. If *the thing* is weather, the writer who says "I saw the storm but it went away" gives his reader too much choice. What storm? A blizzard, an April shower, a welcome rain, or a tornado? The writer who writes "I saw the tern fly away, high on a hunt for fish" or "We saw the squall advance out of the Northwest across the water and were relieved when it veered away from us" focuses the reader's thoughts and directs them, as water is channeled through the narrow end of a funnel. Here are some ways to accumulate and use precise labels:

CATEGORIES

Purpose: accumulation of nouns and adjectives

Description: Start with four categories which are of interest to almost all ages: wildlife, clothing, colors and foods, for instance. Take a piece of paper or an index card and head it with one of the categories. See how many words you can list under it. As you get going, each one will remind you of another and you will be surprised how many you can marshall. For example, using a time limit of one minute per category a first grader and a sixth grader came up with the following lists. The first grader produced:

wildlife*

tiger	horse
kangaroo	cow
elephant	lamb
gerbil	goat
cat	chicken
dog	duck

*Although some of these are not strictly wildlife, they were allowed since the child lived in the city and had no pets.

clothing	*food*
shoes	hamburger
socks	hotdogs
pants	chicken
shirt	steak
skirt	salad
sweater	celery
hat	lettuce
boots	tomatoes
raincoat	cole slaw
mittens	french fries
parka	cake
	pie
colors	ice cream
red	fruit
orange	
yellow	
green	
blue	
purple	
brown	
black	
white	

The sixth grader was shown the first grader's list but was not allowed any repetition.

wildlife	*colors*
armadillo	plaid
ostrich	stripes
skunk	polka dots
possum	lavender
otter	chinese red
racoon	fire engine red
beaver	blood red
muskrat	light gray
mole	charcoal gray
owl	buttercup yellow
rabbit	cornflower
bear	
hedgehog	
fox	

clothing	*food*
bathing suit	lobster
gaiters	pork chops
blue jeans	fish sticks
corduroys	brussels sprouts
turtle neck	asparagus
jacket	broccoli
cowboy boots	cauliflower
knickers	peas
down vest	beans
belt	tarts
bandana	cupcakes
cap	angel food cake
hat	devils food cake
gloves	strawberry shortcake
scarf	mashed potatoes
	baked potatoes

ASSOCIATIONS

Purpose: collating and sorting vocabulary through association

Description: Free association, like categorization, can prove to a participant that he has far more words floating around in his head than he realized. For example, last summer, Ted said to me, "For somebody fifteen I don't have a very big vocabulary. I can't think what to say and lots of times I get tangled up. My Mom says I 'wix my merds'." He was proud and relieved at the following accomplishment. Given sixty seconds to name as many words as possible relating to Bigfoot, he produced:

scary	free
halry	untamed
smelly	sailing
big	good
wild	Oregon
nature	Cascades
primitive	VERY SCARY

Cro-Magnon man	night
evolution	unknown
Darwin	misunderstood
	wonder

As he spoke them, I wrote them down, and he was delighted with the variety and his grand total of twenty-one.

The mention of a specific person, creature, hobby, or profession can release a big flow of related words. For instance, a first grader and a college student, asked for ten words evoked by the word "teacher" produced:

first grader	*college student*
chalk	knowledge
blackboard	generosity
nice	pedagogy
paper	tenure
pencil	discipline
stars	research
smile	library
homework	questions
books	discussions
laughing	grades

Asked to provide a word to pair with the following vocations or avocations, a senior in high school produced:

philatelist . . . perforation	gypsy . . . abduction
orator . . . eloquence	flautist . . . pitch
apiarist . . . sting	alchemist . . . formula
sorcerer . . . incantation	diarist . . . quill

Using these models, ask your students to select some additional categories and develop them in similar ways.

MIX AND MATCH

Purpose: combining labels to expand expressive capacity
Description: Make two lists, one of verbs and the other of
  nouns depicting emotions. Begin with familiar
  combinations and try to develop some originals.

Verb	*With*	*Emotions*
quiver	with	anticipation
dance	with	joy
chortle	with	glee
jump	with	guilt
fill	with	happiness
burn	with	rage
rage	wlth	passion
overflow	with	tenderness
howl	with	pain
soar	with	inspiration

Here are some to be finished:

wobble	with	_____
expound	with	_____
meander	with	_____
tremble	with	_____
sizzle	with	_____
squirt	with	_____
startle	with	_____

or

_____	with	terror
_____	with	revulsion
_____	with	discouragement
_____	with	elation
_____	with	apprehension
_____	with	bitterness
_____	with	puzzlement

INITIALLY YOURS

Purpose: assembling and playing with many adverbs and adjectives

Description: Give each participant an index card or piece of paper for each initial in his name. On each one he should list as many adjectives and adverbs (nouns, too, if he likes) beginning with those letters. From these lists he will make a description of himself which will be flattering, satirical or honest. For example:

David	*Lincoln*	*Smith*
Daring	Likeable	Smart
Delightful	Lazy	Sunny
Dashing	Loony	Sensible
Devilish	Libelous	Sensitive
Disorderly	Lean	Spectacular
Devastating	Lovely	Sarcastic

Through transmogrification this hapless fellow could be known to be *Disorderly, Lazy* and *Sarcastic* or a *Daring Likeable Spirit. William Anderson Southwick* became a *Wonderfully Amiable Soul, Robert Ryan Reilly* a *Rebellious Roaring Rooster* and *James Edgar Jones* a *Jester, Ever Just.* If I am occasionally *Plump, Lallygagging,* and *Voluble,* what are you?

AN EXULTATION OF LARKS, OR RUBBER RUBRICS

Purpose: playing with and inventing the terminology of plurals and combinations

Description: Begin with the familiar...

a pride of lions
a brace of pheasants
a herd of sheep
a flock of geese

and invent some new ones...

a dazzle of daughters
a drone of headaches
a semester of questions

Here are some starters...

a _____ of squid
a _____ of weeds
a _____ of ideas

or...

a stickiness of _____
a discrimination of _____
a felicity of _____

The writer with a scintillation of labels will produce a startle of combinations!

What is the purpose of such listings? The simple process of sorting words into categories makes them more accessible when a writer needs them. Collecting related words through exercises such as these gives the writer an orderly supply from which to choose the one which most precisely matches his intention. Lists of words with personal appeal to the writer can be kept in a special notebook. Encourage your students to explore additional categories or new associations. Labels are like the narrow end of a funnel; they direct the flow of a reader's thoughts.

OCTOBER: BEASTS

Purpose: exploring and extending the topic of great beasts
Description: October is an ideal month for strange beasts and mythical creatures: days shorten, darkness encroaches foreshadowing winter, and monsters and goblins cavort on Halloween.

As an introduction to the topic ask your students to collect some information on such huge creatures as mammoths, albatrosses, whales, elephants, or dinosaurs. There may be others they want to add to the list, or perhaps they would rather investigate animals whose habits are less generally known (armadillos, aardvarks, llamas, ostriches) or are misunderstood like the wolf, whose reputation for cruelty and violence is undeserved.

Students of all ages enjoy inventing their own beasts. The caliber of their work and the power of their imaginings will increase in the wake of studying another genus or two. Begin with dinosaurs. Being gigantic, widely varied, extinct and therefore somewhat mysterious, dinosaurs are ideal subjects for studying important and distinguishing characteristics. For example, Tyrannosaurus Rex, which walked on its hind legs and flashed its teeth was an aggressive fighter. Brontosaurus lumbered on all fours through the swamps, a gentle vegetarian. Triceratops' form might represent the imaginings of a mad inventor. High school students offered the following descriptions of these three dinosaur species:

Tyrannosaurus Rex: fierce, guards his territorial rights, ruthless, attacks without warning and sometimes without provocation

Brontosaurus: vulnerable, guileless, clumsy and gentle, like Ferdinand the Bull or Beauty's Beast, a pussycat at heart

Triceratops: like a rhinoceros, he's bad tempered and tricky. Untrustworthy creatures, like untrustworthy people, are dangerous in the home.

While the dinosaurs seemed to be different in disposition they all shared great size and all were covered with a strange kind of skin.

It is but a short step from these extinct creatures to those that may or may not exist such as the Loch Ness Monster and Big Foot. Guide your students to research both sides of the question and to hear or read the evidence which purports to prove each point of view. Having moved from actual beasts, extinct or not, to questionable beasts, your students will be ready for legendary or mythical beasts. Here are five they can learn about:

The griffin: a mythical animal with the head and wings of an eagle and the body of a lion

The phoenix: a mythical bird which consumed itself in fire and rose from its own ashes, thereby symbolizing immortality

The unicorn: a mythical horse-like white animal with a single spiralled horn growing from the center of its forehead; reputed to be gentle, vulnerable, and graceful; has appeared in poetry, tapestry, and legend

The centaur: a creature from Greek mythology possessing the arms, trunk, and head of a man with the body and legs of a horse

The minotaur: a monster from Greek mythology with the body of a man and the head of a bull (reversed in some versions) which inhabited a labyrinth on Crete and was fed an annual feast of seven maidens and seven youths until Theseus slew him

Either a rich background of information or a nodding acquaintance with legendary creatures prepares a writer to create his own: naming it, drawing its portrait, cataloguing such information as its habitat, food, natural enemies, quirks, and adventures. Rather than my saying this can be done, however, let me introduce the Strepawhib, the Grumasplin and the Empospond, progeny of three fourth-grade boys.

The Strepawhib

The Strepawhib has two hairy red wings, an eagle-like head with three spotty eyes, a wobbly body, and a nose like a crocodile. He lives in a dark dungeon. There are lots of cells. The Strepawhib hides in a long corridor and when people walk by he grabs them and puts them in cells.

The Strepawhib's enemy is the Hornswoggle because he eats the Strepawhib's people. When they meet, the Strepawhib spits fire at him, but then the Hornswoggle spits freeze-ray at the Strepawhib. Here are his favorite foods:

vegetables	sauerkraut
meat	cockroach legs
fruit	hollow apples with worms
dessert	blueberry bears with worm sauce (warm)

He invited me over for dinner, but I said no thanks!

The Grumasplin

Introducing the Grumasplin who has:

14 fuzzy green hairs
a head made out of a blue fork
4 1/2 ears
a 12-inch orange tail
a pouch and stripes
6 purple and pink striped eyes
banana legs
4 arms

The Grumasplin lives in a very strange country. It is half bad and half good. On the good side there are flowers and green grass, butterflies and bees, kites and trees. On the bad side there are flying tarantulas, dead trees, caves with bats, and other creepy things. He goes back and forth.

The Empospond

Here is an Empospond. He has seven spotted tusks, one eyeball, and one hairy eyebrow. He lives on a desert island which is big and has lots of sharp cactuses. When he steps on them it does not hurt because he has rough feet. He lives in a building under the sand. It has 1000 rooms and an elevator that goes every which way. Half of it is under the sea, and there are strong windows in each room so the Empospond can stick his spikey tongue out at the fish.

His natural enemy is a two-headed gorilla. Whenever they meet they fight and fight and fight! His best friend is a Mazokeen. A Mazokeen is an elf with wings, and it can turn into any shape it wants.

The invention of these three creatures marked the beginning of an independent writing project that lasted eight weeks—investigating other mighty creatures, imagining new adventures for each beast, and combining art work and humor with writing.

If your students want to read some books about other creatures (before or while working on their own) here is a very brief list:

My Mama Says There Aren't Any Zombies, Ghosts, Vampires, Creatures, Demons, Monsters, Fiends, Goblins or Things by Judith Viorst, Atheneum.
Dragons by Peter Hogarth and Val Clery. A Studio Book, Viking Press.
Bulfinch's Mythology. A Studio Book, Viking Press.
The First Book of Legendary Beings, by Helen Jacobson. Franklin Watts.
Dragons, Unicorns and Other Magical Beasts, by Robin Palmer. Henry Z. Walck.
A Dictionary of Mythical Places, by Robin Palmer. Henry Z. Walck.

NOVEMBER: IF

Purpose: Pretending in writing
Description: A kingdom of verbal abstraction rests on the two-letter word *if*. Unobtrusive in size and sound, taken for granted by those who understand It, *if* seldom receives its rightful share of glory.

The ability to understand *if* is one of the distinctions separating the language humans use among one another from the language humans use in speaking to animals. The dog, the primate, and the dolphin may respond appropriately to "sit," "Nim likes bananas," or "Swim for the dime." But not even Flipper understands the subjunctive. *If* is a *passe-partout*, a key of universal access to the realm of hypothesis.

From a limitless number of possibilities, here are some examples of student work resting on *if*s:

If I were another person
If I were a place
If I were a thing

If I Were Another Person

If I was a king I would ask my builder to build me a castle. I would give him $100 in cash. I would be broke forever, but I would be happy.

Kyle Rawlins　Grade 1

I am a king. I can boss you around. "So go! I am angry. I will cut off your head." "Oh, no, sorry! I over reacted".

Luke Wasserman　Grade 1

I am a good queen and sometimes I get angry. I stamp my foot and my face gets red. The king tells me to take a nap. He says, "It will help you."

Shalli Starr　Grade 1

If I Were a Place

Earth

I am earth.
I spin around the sun and moon.
It takes a year to spin all the way around.
I am colorful.
I am big.
I go around fast.

Brian Dawson　Grade 1

Sea

If I were the sea I would always have tickling in my stomach from the fish swimming back and forth. I would be able to have sand between my toes the whole year 'round, and I would always have a fluffy springy hairdo from the wind whipping my waves into shape. But with all that seaweed, I would have trouble shaving my legs!

Rachel Waters　Grade 8

Air

If I were air, I would be invisible but powerful. I would surround airplanes, be hospitable to birds, and house the wind. Clouds would cool me, and I would be warmed by the land. Thunderstorms would be painful, the lightning would rip me like a knife. I would bring both good and bad to the earth with neither pride nor remorse. I would be eternal.

Thomas Eliot   Grade 11

If I Were a Thing (visible)

The Life of A Ball

I'm a ball. I get bounced all over
the place. Sometimes I am hit with
sticks and bats but I don't mind
because kids have fun with me.

by David Thorn   grade 3

If I Were a Thing (invisible)

The Difficulty and Joys of Being a Voice

One day I was in my sister's mouth. She shouted very loud and threw me off tone. So evidently my sister lost her voice. I guess she didn't like me because she tried to drown me in salt water. That night she was brushing her teeth. It was like a minty bubble to me. One of the sad parts of being a voice is having a sore throat. Another difficulty of being a voice is operas. They will strain and tire your sound.

The reason I advise you not to be a voice is you never know what key will be hit.

Lori Atkins   grade 3

Here are some samples to try:

If I were a piece of furniture, I would be _____ because . . .
If I were a kind of food, I would be _____ because . . .
If I were a flower, I would be a _____ because . . .

If I were an animal, I would be a _____ because . . .
If I were an appliance, I would be a _____ because . . .
If I were a musical instrument, I would be a _____
because . . .

If I could have my way, all students would have daily
opportunities to reach into their imaginations and put
their discoveries on paper. If you want to give your
students this kind of exercise without draining too
much time away from other academic pursuits, try
posting a daily *If* to be used as a story-starter for
individual work or a warm-up to get a group lesson
going. Encourage brief but vivid responses.

DECEMBER: HOLIDAYS

Purpose: celebrating, describing and inventing reasons to
rejoice

Description: Societies and cultures that may differ from one
another in time, place, and ambiance frequently share
traditions for ceremony and celebration. Holidays at
harvest time are very common as are ceremonies to
mark the return of spring. Many cluster around the
autumnal and vernal equinox. Suggest to your students
that they proceed as follows.

Get or make a calendar for the next twelve months.
Start with the month you are in now. Ideally, give each
month a page of its own. Save room at the top, or on a
facing page for an illustration (either a drawing or a
picture cut from a magazine) of any of the holidays in
the month. Be sure to mark your own birthday and any
other days which are personally important as well as
local or regional holidays. Here are some traditional
holidays to get you going:

September: Labor Day
Rosh Hoshana
Yom Kippur
First Day of Autumn

October:	Columbus Day
	Hallowe'en
November:	Election Day
	Veteran's Day
	Thanksgiving
December:	St. Lucia's Day
	First Day of Winter
	Hanukkah
	Christmas
	New Year's Eve
January:	New Year's Day
	Martin Luther King's Birthday
February:	Groundhog Day
	Valentine's Day
	Washington's Birthday
March:	St. Patrick's Day
	First Day of Spring
	Passover (March or April)
	Easter (March or April)
April:	April Fool's Day
	Income Tax Day
May:	Memorial Day
June:	Flag Day
	First Day of Summer
July:	Independence Day
August:	Women's Equality Day

Once your students have included the traditional holidays on their calendars, ask each student to create a new one. He must decide when it should be, where and how it might have originated, what type of celebration should mark it, what particular color or type of costume should be worn and why, and any special kind of food which should be eaten. Ask each student to write a letter to the editor of the local newspaper explaining why this holiday should be celebrated nationally or at least regionally. Each participant should design a greeting card announcing the new holiday and send it to a friend. Students will enjoy marking their friends' new holidays on their own personal calendars.

In addition each student can select a holiday with customs that are generally familiar and make a booklet about it, first describing it factually and then writing a myth describing its origin. For example, a high school student chose Valentine's Day. On the cover she made a heart-shaped collage of paper lace, snippets of actual valentines and the type of inscriptions which adorn pastel candy hearts: "you're for me," "you bet," "wise guy," and "be mine." Inside she wrote a description of the holiday and its customs in a letter to a visitor from Mars. Then she wrote a myth explaining its origin. She described how, long ago, a plague of type L&L virus called Loneliness-and-Lackluster traditionally followed the annual January flu epidemic. This L&L plague characterized the entire month of February. Sages and doctors tried to eradicate it with no success. Finally, a family of children, convalescing from the flu and under strict instructions to be quiet, tidy, and shy in matters of romance, disobeyed all three admonitions and vanquished the virus with valentines.

JANUARY: DESCRIPTION

Purpose: practicing different kinds of description
Description: Discuss with your class some of the tools used for descriptive writing. For instance, in straightforward description of sensory images a skillful writer uses nouns and strong verbs to evoke clear pictures, and may choose to add adjectives and adverbs as ornaments. In more oblique description a writer uses comparison, relying on terms of *degree*, *simile*, *analogy* and *metaphor*. Poetic description may be either straightforward or symbolic.

Assuring your students that their descriptive attempts may be kept private will encourage bold experimentation. To get going, ask each student to choose a sample of his physical surroundings or a recent experience and decide whether it seems best suited to sensory images, comparison or poetry. Then try it. If it doesn't work, no one need ever know. Throw it away and try another topic or a different treatment. The important thing is to try. Here are some samples.

Sensory Images

Eschewing adjectives or adverbs, Adam (age sixteen) made this entry of straight sensory description in his journal:

Camping

I see fireflies and the silhouettes of hemlocks in the New Hampshire evenings. I hear the calls of loons and water lapping at the shore of the lake. I smell pine-needles and the campfire as I feel its warmth and sift a handful of soil. I taste a piece of grass and prepare for sleep.

These first graders added adjectives.

The World

I like all the flowers
And the shining water
And all the lovely things
In the world.

Robert Gold

Me and My Bed

I have a crayon bed with paper as the sheets, and with lots of colors—yellow, orange, red, green, purple, blue, brown, black and white. They are big crayons. They always poke me. They hurt me. I wish I had another bed. I wish it would be bouncy. I like bouncy beds. They are fun to play in. It is fun to jump high. I like to jump up and hit the ceiling. I jump every day before I go to bed. I do it night and morning.

Brian Dawson

If your students need to expand their supplies of adjectives and adverbs, encourage them to make an individual or group *Alphabet Soup*. Begin by collecting one adjective and adverb for each letter of the alphabet.

They needn't tie in with one another, the purpose is to develop a catalogue. Here is a sample beginning.

Alphabet Soup

adjective	*adverb*
agile	adversely
bombastic	barely
cantankerous	candidly
dutiful	doubly
eager	easily
fortunate	fiercely
gorgeous	gladly
hateful	happily
ignorant	ineptly
joyous	jealously
knobby	kiddingly
luminous	lightly
moonlit	merrily
negative	noisily
open	outrageously
practical	pompously
querulous	quietly
restless	rudely
sunny	sadly
troublesome	tightly
understandable	unsuspectingly
venomous	vividly
wicked	weakly
xanthic	xenophobically
young	yieldingly
zealous	zippily

Comparison

Degree, simile, analogy and *metaphor* are four ways to describe through comparison.

Terms of *degree* (the endings *er* and *est*) are efficient ways to contrast things or people with one another: Jack is big, but Fred is bigger, and Alan is the biggest of all. Many adjectives lend themselves to endings of degree. Here are some for your students to experiment with: fine, tiny, loud, near, low, soft, quiet, lumpy. Add others as they occur to the group and leave room to enjoy an occasional aberration as I did when five-year-old Angus turned a noun into an adjective saying, "Amanda is the queenest of all!" Ask your students to select a term of degree and use it as a story starter: The Quietest Thing.

Simile compares things with one another using the pattern "as _____ as _____." As mean as a snake, as warm as sunshine, and as pretty as a picture are all as old as the hills. Here are twenty other starters for your students to complete:

as sharp as _____
as deep as _____
as smooth as _____
as welcome as _____
as soft as _____
as tiny as _____
as angry as _____
as happy as _____
as hot as _____
as perfect as _____
as rough as _____
as sweet as _____
as brown as _____
as high as _____
as wild as _____
as slippery as _____
as loud as _____
as gentle as _____
as turbulent as _____
as melodic as _____

Obvious and familiar completions will pop to mind. To avoid the temptation to use them exclusively, try to think of three completions for each phrase. For example, two six year old boys produced these: as quiet as fog, as quiet as a stone and as quiet as one hundred tiny spies on the run. Variety is welcome. The writer who uses trite simile will run into a reader or an editor who is as cold as charity.

Ask your students to select three similes and use each one as the topic sentence of a paragraph or the title of a story they will write.

Analogy sets up parallel comparisons. Use it to describe your setting and what you are doing at the moment. Analogy can express many ideas in a mere four words. For example as I am writing this on our porch, the carpenter, Mike Lawless, is putting a new section of roof on our house. Thus

> Mike : hammer :: Priscilla : pencil
> hammer : roof :: pencil : chapter
> roof : house :: chapter : book

Analogy is not reserved for adults. Some young children use it adeptly as two of my third grade students, Andrew and Bill, did when they produced these:

> men : apes :: Dr. Jekyll : Mr. Hyde
> food : hunger :: talk : curiosity

Here are some half-completed analogies for you to try with your students:

> _____ : _____ :: student : classroom
> _____ : _____ :: teacher : student
> _____ : _____ :: paper : notebook
> _____ : _____ :: ideas : books
> _____ : _____ :: dictionary : student
> _____ : _____ :: bike : school bus
> _____ : _____ :: pass : fail

Ask your students to use analogy as a way of writing puzzles for one another, as topic sentences of paragraphs or titles of essays. Once an idea is encapsulated in an analogy it is good practice to expand it in prose.

Metaphor describes through implied comparison. Shakespeare gave us "all the world's a stage" and Emily Dickinson described parting as "all we need of hell." Here are some other personal favorites of mine which you may enjoy discussing with your students. T.S. Eliot commented on the human condition "we are but balloons dancing in a land of pins," an employer describing a dilletantish employee said "She is a dragonfly, approaching with great whirring of wings, rippling the surface of the water momentarily, and then vanishing." In writing about health Norman Cousins said "laughter is internal jogging," and a disillusioned eleventh grader wrote "first love is a honey bee with a stinger!" Here are some for your students to experiment with:

Graduation is (a) _____
Friendship is (a) _____
Windows are (the) _____
Mudpuddles are (the) _____
_____ is a magic carpet.
_____ is (are) a shower of fireworks.
_____ are the tall ships under sail.
_____ become the rainbow after the storm.
_____ is home for the heart.

Ask each student to select a metaphor and write a descriptive passage leading up to it, using the metaphor as the punch line.

Here are three metaphoric riddles. Can your students answer them?* Can they invent new ones?

I am a bonnet for the earth, dotted with clover, green, and soft as velvet. I am _____ .

I am a vise around the heart, invisible, intangible but recognizeable. At one time or another I have walked with everyone. I am _____ .

I am a tingle, an itch, an explosion. If you try too hard to catch me, I run away and hide. I am a _____ .

Poetic Description

Poetry can incorporate all kinds of description from sensory imagery to simile and metaphor as these three

*answers: grass, fear, a sneeze.

examples illustrate. In the following Haiku a fifteen year old girl describes an early evening shower.

Soft rain falls gently
Quietly soothing the thirst
Of twilight flowers

William Wordsworth used both sensory imagery and simile in describing his springtime amble which begins:

"I wandered lonely as a cloud . . ."

Poetic description may give the writer a way of weaving together simple and complex ideas in a relatively few words, with the poem becoming a metaphor in and of itself. When William Butler Yeats, in *The Lake Isle of Innisfree*, writes of his intention to arise and go to Innisfree he is specific in his description of the concrete surroundings he expects to have, yet many readers find the poem a metaphor for a spiritual journey to inner tranquility rather than a physical journey to a particular place. Few are the writers with Yeats' capacity for such symbolic description, but any writer who wants to try deserves encouragement.

Ask each student to pick a person, an article of clothing or a recent event and describe it in poetry. As mentioned in the beginning of this section, assurance of privacy will encourage boldness of attempt.

These examples do not pretend to encompass perfection, but the variety illustrates how many ways there are to describe simple or familiar situations. The important thing for the writer is frequent practice, familiarity with different kinds of construction and plenty of chances to experiment with them.

FEBRUARY: FAIRY TALES

Purpose: reading and writing fairy tales
Description: If the winter doldrums are upon you and you

yearn for a treat, a vacation, or a change, remember that universally accessible and refreshing watering spot "Once-a-pond-a time." Fairy tales are stories of wish-fulfillment. Sometimes the happy ending is attributable to magic, sometimes to cleverness, and sometimes because right makes might, but whatever the reason, the good always triumphs in fairy tales, and in the end "they lived happily ever after."

These stories tell of *innocence,* a *threat, allies* whose powers are concealed, a *confrontation,* a *timely rescue* and the wish-fulfillment of a *happy ending.* The story of *Snow White* exemplifies this pattern. Innocence is represented by the loving and beautiful princess who is threatened by her jealous, murderous step-mother. Through the story she is saved and befriended by allies who do not initially appear to be prepossessing, royal or powerful; a common huntsman, the birds and small animals of the forest, and seven little men. At the confrontation the step-mother appears in disguise, and Snow White, guileless and trusting, suspects no evil in her visitor. Her rescue happens in two stages. First the dwarfs guard her sleeping, seemingly lifeless form in its glass casket, and second the prince arrives to awaken her with love's first kiss, after which he takes her away on his horse in total wish-fulfillment to live happily ever after.

The plot of *Sleeping Beauty* contains the same elements. *Beauty and the Beast, Cinderella, The Princess on the Glass Hill* and *Puss in Boots* are a few others which are built on the same patterns. Actually, *Jane Eyre* is much the same story with adult rather than magical characters.

The best way for your students to start writing fairy tales is to hear them and read them first. Start with any or all of the ones mentioned above or others which are personal favorites of yours. As you read aloud to your group, or while they are reading to themselves, ask them to listen for these six elements: *innocence, threat, allies, confrontation,* the *timely rescue* and the *happy ending.*

Then take six cups or paper bags, one for each element. Give your students slips of paper or index cards and ask them to write characters or incidents for each category. (See some suggestions below) Each student then draws one slip from each container and combines the elements in an original fairy tale. It doesn't matter if more than one person draws a particular paper. Here are some starters:

The Innocent One (who is almost always impoverished, is frequently motherless or an orphan)

a lonely traveller
a homeless dog
a beautiful young girl
the unwitting possessor of a secret
a baby abandoned in a basket
a boy in an orphanage

The Threat

a jealous relative
an evil old man
someone whose fortunes would be ruined by the disclosure of the secret
a malevolent sorceress
a cruel holder of power
a tempter

The Allies (frequently appear to be weak, ineffectual or physically stunted or misshapen, sometimes they are animals)

a small boy
a blind girl
three children
an animal who had once been helped by the innocent one
an old, bent woman
an elf, dwarf or gnome

The Confrontation
bodily ambush
trickery and poison

imprisonment
transformation by magic spell
seduction through temptation to join the forces of evil

The Timely Rescue

a brother on horseback
a handsome prince
transformation by magic spell
the power of clever thinking
sudden arrival of an agent of good, frequently over
   water or out of the air

The Happy Ending

acquisition of land, wealth, power and love
love, marriage and descendants
detailed destruction of evil and crowning of good
escape and freedom
acquisition of magic powers

Keep adding new ideas to each category. There is an almost endless variety of stories which can result from even such a slender beginning as this. Of course a student may invent all six elements for his own story, he needn't be restricted to the containers. Here is one of my favorites written by a girl in fifth grade who has included all six elements though not in the exact sequence suggested above.

The Traveler

There once was a traveler on horseback—weary, thirsty, and with no prospect of shelter. He rode along and along until through the shadows of the early evening he saw the shape of a castle ahead. Comforted, he guided his horse in that direction. When he arrived, he tethered his horse and walked inside. No one was there. It seemed spooky, but he was glad to be indoors where he could relax and so he fell asleep.

When he woke up it was midnight, and there was wild revelry. Hags, vultures and creatures were dancing to a wild tune. The traveler looked and was afraid. He looked for the door, but for a long time he couldn't find it. Then he found it, but it was locked and there was no knob on the inside. He was trapped. Again he was afraid.

Then came the dawn. Through the dusty window came a sunbeam. It looked like a road to the traveler and so he stepped on it and walked on it out through the window and to his tethered horse which he released, and they rode away together.

MARCH: POETRY

Purpose: writing different kinds of poetry
Description: Here are some patterns for poetry to add to the suggestions in earlier sections. A teacher can use them with a whole class, small groups or individual students.

One of a Kind

People can be proud of the features which make them unique. Each person's eyes are different and expressive, as are their hands and fingerprints. The same is true of mouths. These features can be the subjects of *One of a Kind* poems. Ask each student to write a poem about someone's eyes using at least two adjectives and whatever rhyme scheme appeals to him. Here is an example:

Brown Eyes

Brown is warm
Brown is kind
Looking in brown eyes I find
Strength and laughter underlined.

Ask each student to write a cinquain (see page 135) about his own hand and encircle it with a border of his fingerprints or a drawing of a mitten. Here is an example:

Hand
sturdy   gentle
making things, waving to people, holding
small   clean
individual

Ask your students to write about someone's mouth. Here is an example:

> You've lips that can whistle
> And pucker and smack,
> When I give you my smile
> They send me yours back.

Or they may prefer to write of the songs which can come from a mouth as these fourth, fifth and sixth graders did as part of Project R.E.A.D. (Reading Enrichment Through Art and Drama) at a public school in New York City.*

> I sing of red roses turning into rainbows
> I sing of shining hours glowing on a rose
> I sing of dreams I never forget
> I sing of a dragon with the sun in his mouth.

Your class can write a group poem if each member contributes one line beginning with *I sing of*... When all the entries are in, arrange them in a manner which pleases the aesthetic sense of the group, ask one person to transcribe it and post it on the bulletin board.

Sense Poems

Write a phrase containing "as _____ as" which matches each of the five senses. Use each phrase as the title of a poem and write the poem to go with it. Here are five sample phrases in which possible titles are underlined.

> Seeing: As pretty as the morning sun on the harbor
> Hearing: As scary as a creaking door at midnight
> Smelling: As inviting as the smell of baking cake
> Tasting: As comforting as chicken broth
> Touching: As scratchy as Harris tweed

Color Poems

Choose a color. Write one line for each thing the

*as reported in the New York Times, June 13, 1979

color reminds you of, followed by a line of one adjective.
Example:

Gray

Gray is an old lady's dress
Shabby
Gray is a sky full of rain
Dreary
Gray is an elephant's hide
Wrinkled
Gray is a shadow
Substanceless
Gray is the fog
Enveloping

Wh Poems

Write the six *wh* words (who, what, when, where, why,
how) on the board as a reminder of the categories they
represent and ask each student to choose one and
write a poem to accompany it. Here is an example
written by an eighteen-year-old poet in England who
prefers to remain anonymous.

When

When did my childhood go
Was it the day I ceased to be eleven
Was it the day I realized that Hell and Heaven
Could not be found in Geography
And therefore could not be,
Was that the day?

When did my childhood go
Was it the time I realized that adults were not all they
    seemed to be
They talked of love and preached of love
But did not act so lovingly
Was that the day?

When did my childhood go
Was it the day I found my mind was really mine
To use whichever way I choose

Producing thoughts that were not those of other people
But mine and mine alone
Was that the day?

Where did my childhood go
It went to some forgotten place
That's hidden in an infant's face
That's all I know.

Three Lines

This is a pattern used by Marylea Franz in her kindergarten class in our school which has also been used with adults in teacher training seminars. It is equally successful with both age groups and all the levels in between. Here is the recipe:

1st line: three words
2nd line: repeat 1st line and add one word
3rd line: remove first word and add a new word at the
    end.

Here are some examples of kindergarten work.

Pointed tall castles
Pointed tall castles stand
Tall castles stand proudly.

Soft white clouds
Soft white clouds move
White clouds move slowly.

Mushy brown mud
Mushy brown mud bubbles
Brown mud bubbles when you step in it.

Hungry white ghost
Hungry white ghost howls
White ghost howls in the night.

Anticipation.

Expectation—either of a doomsday event such as a dreaded exam or of a happy occasion such as a birthday—is part of everyone's experience. Ask each student to write a poem describing a personal example of anticipation. Here is an example written by a fourth grade girl.

Spring at Last

All this winter dark and long
I've never heard a bird in song
Nor felt green grass beneath my feet
Or smelled a flower soft and sweet
I've never seen a tree's green crown
Or dug in soil soft and brown
But I have longed for a certain thing
I have longed and yearned for spring.

Christina Rae

APRIL: BIOGRAPHY

Purpose: organizing and presenting factual information
Description: The writer who enjoys working with factual material will welcome biography; collecting, sorting, arranging and presenting objective and subjective information. The writer may want to present a straight biographical study of one person or may choose to write a biography contrasting the lives of two people. The older student may enjoy researching information in the library, while the younger or less-experienced student may prefer to write about people he can interview. Here are suggestions and samples to help your students write biographies of figures from the past, people living now and groups of people who share a common interest or pursuit.

Figures from the Past. The prospect of writing a biography of a famous person may seem an intimidating or exhausting task to the novice, but here are some suggestions to get things off to a good start.

First of all point out that biographies can be of people who worked in many different fields. Elicit some categories from your students: politicians, authors, composers, artists, explorers, heros, martyrs, and athletes to name a few. When the categories are established, elicit names of people who belong under each of the headings. The fact that the categories and people have come from the students themselves indicates that these are pursuits and people of interest to your burgeoning biographers. Then brainstorm, asking what kind of information a straight biographical study should include. Encourage them to combine objective and subjective information and to include some human interest about the subject in addition to reciting dates and accomplishments. What set this person apart from others? What links him to his time? Why is he an outstanding subject? Why should people know about him? If he were to reappear today how might he feel about current issues? Where did he live . . . not just his address, but a description of his surroundings.

Next discuss how to obtain the necessary information. If you have a well-stocked library in your school, do your students know how to use it? Is there a town library they can use in addition or instead? Should they get their information from encyclopedias and book-length biographies? Is it feasible for them to investigate some primary sources?

Finally decide with your group how long and how detailed the biographies should be. Strike a realistic agreement with them and keep the project in manageable proportions.

If you feel they are ready, explore the idea of a comparative biographical study in which the student chooses a category, selects two people from it and contrasts their lives. This can be done by writing an introduction explaining what the figures have in common and why it is interesting to pair and contrast them. Then follows a biography of each and finally a conclusion which ties the comparison together.

For example, a tenth-grade boy wrote a comparative study titled *Men of Music; Mozart and Lennon*. In his introduction he explained that these were two men who wrote beautiful music and had a profound influence even though they lived short lives. The he wrote an individual biography of each man discussing the following topics: how long he lived, the family he grew up in, when his talent and interest first showed, how he studied and learned music, his first opportunity to perform, the reaction of the public and its effect on the composer, his emotional life (marriage, close relationships etc.) significant cultural forces of his time, the writer's assessment of how such forces influenced the musician and how the influence showed (sounded) in his work, the cause of his early death, and the magnitude and texture of his contribution. The conclusion wove the two stories together. As an extra he attached a cassette of music by each for the reader to hear.

People Living Now. Follow the same procedure for getting started; choose categories, list people who fit them, discuss sources of information and agree on the magnitude of the final product. Students can choose subjects who are famous, at a distance, little-known, or nearby. They may get their information from libraries or through interviews. As with figures from the past they may choose to write a straight or comparative study. For example, a fifth-grade girl decided to write parallel biographies of a classmate and a teacher who happened to share the name Christina. She discovered that, although the two Christinas were born in different years, they were both born in November; both were Scorpios who shared a topaz as a birthstone. Both were born on the East Coast in an even numbered year. Neither one inherited the name from family connections; their mothers chose it for its lyric quality. Each Christina was the oldest in her family. One confessed to being afraid of spiders or of capsizing in a sailboat. The other feared high places and waking in the middle of the night in an unfamiliar place. Given a choice between reading poetry or mysteries, each one chose differently, but given a choice between chocolate mousse and strawberry shortcake, both chose the latter. One Christina loved yellow, the other purple. The junior biographer collected her information, presented it in a booklet with photographs of each as the frontispiece, and made a cover for the booklet by writing their names as a crossword—one in yellow, the other in purple.

```
                    C
                    h
                    r
                    i
          Christina
                    t
                    i
                    n
                    a
```

Groups of People. There are some students who enjoy finding out about other people but who feel overwhelmed at the prospect of writing a prose biography. Such students may welcome group biography as an alternative. Having been allowed to begin writing biography this way they may not be afraid to tackle subsequent assignments.

In many ways a school year-book is a biography of a group. Usually offering a photograph of each member of the graduating class, each individual's statistics and story are told in a common format. Such information as: name, nickname, address, year of entry at school, extracurricular activities, offices held, and perhaps next destination. Often the punch-line is a quotation chosen by the subject. Rifling the pages it is easy to get a sense of the group. If the year-book format appeals to a

student or a group of students, they can use it to
describe and contrast the members of almost any group
from a particular class to the student government
officers, the cast of a play or an athletic team.
Photographs may or may not present a problem. If they
are hard to obtain, omit them. The important thing is for
the student or students to reach a consensus on what
information is to be included and how it should be laid
out in a systematic and appealing way.

A more unusual approach to biographies of groups
is to ask your students to adopt the baseball card
format. Though baseball cards are usually banned in
classrooms, their format can serve a student well as an
entertaining and instructive way to present a good deal
of information in a small space. Never mind that it will be
given in rows, columns and abbreviations rather than in
prose paragraphs. This is exactly the kind of relief you
are trying to give a reluctant student. Here is a way to
begin and an example.

With your group or individual student select the
group to be described and decide what information it is
important to gather and present. Then rank the items in
order of importance and devise some abbreviations.
Provide index cards. A photograph, illustration or logo
can go on the blank side of the card and the information
on the lined side.

An eleventh-grade girl chose the card format as a
way of analyzing and comparing the make up of the U.S.
Supreme Court at three times in American history. She
chose the Burger Court, the Warren Court and one of
the courts in which Oliver Wendell Holmes served. The
statistics she chose to compile and present on each of
the nine judges in each of the three courts were:

date of birth
age at date of appointment to the S.C.
political party
judicial philosophy (liberal, conservative)
number of years served on the S.C.
law school
college

three words to describe his personality
family facts
major decisions made by the S.C. during his term on
the bench

MAY: AUTOBIOGRAPHY

Purpose: writing personal description
Description: Persons of all ages enjoy writing
autobiographies. Encouraging a reflective view of one's
own life, this exercise legitimizes the interest we all
have in ourselves. Like other biographies, these will be
more interesting to write and to read if they combine
objective and subjective information.

Shouldn't autobiography come *before* biography of
other people instead of being a follow-up? Not in my
opinion. The critical, evaluative experience of studying
other people—the chronology of their lives, their
passions, successes, failures, the influences which
shaped them and the ways in which they left their mark
on the world—helps the student select and sift the
items and events he needs to tell his own tale. The
student who has read and written biographies of others
can join a noble tradition when he turns his hand to
writing about himself.

Furthermore, as autobiography is a natural
outgrowth of biography, it is an ideal preliminary to
journal-keeping, the subject of the June section.
Sharpening the writer's self-knowledge and providing
opportunities for putting revelations on paper
intensifies the author's awareness of the importance
and impact of his everyday experiences.

In spite of its value, many students are afraid to
tackle autobiography and need to be shown how to
begin. Experience has taught me that the way to tempt
a young, timid or inexperienced writer to start an
autobiography is to make it seem easy, to provide many
opportunities for the writer to express his personal
preferences and to contribute factual information about

himself without having to worry about organization. Help your students assemble a *Me, Myself and I* book. Sample pages are suggested here which provide outlines. They merely require the author to fill in the blanks. Students who have enjoyed completing such sample pages will often invent new ones, and their books will gradually swell and expand as Japanese compressed paper flowers do when they are dropped in a glass of water.

In addition, students who have used such a format to organize and present information about themselves will feel comfortable tackling free form autobiography later on. Whether such an autobiography is a continuation of the pages begun here or a separate endeavor does not matter. The important thing is the ease and skill with which the student approaches the task.

Give each student construction paper for front and back covers, two notebook rings and some sample pages to start the project moving. Here are ten examples:

Page 1. (Leave space for a photograph and lines for the author's name and date.)

Page 2. Vital statistics

I was born_____   _____

        where   when

                  to

_____   _____

        father   mother

I have _____ sisters, _____ brothers,

     _____ aunts, _____ uncles,

          _____ cousins.

These are the names of my Grandparents

Mother's mother   _____

Mother's father   _____

Father's mother   _____

Father's father   _____

Page 3. Playing Favorites

My favorite

    food is _____

    color is _____

    baseball team is _____

    television program is _____

    piece of music is _____

    sport is _____

    book is _____

Here are three other favorites

_____

_____

_____

Page 4. Fingerprints

This is my right thumbprint

This is my left thumbprint

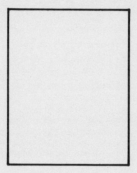

(see earlier section, page 66 on fingerprinting to analyze the prints.)

Each person's fingerprints are unique. No one else in the world has identical ones. Here are some other things that are unique about me:

Pages 5, 6, 7, 8. Follow in identical framework for the four seasons. Here is one page:

In the summer I go _____

_____

This is what I like to do, and here is a drawing of how I look. (Leave a generous space for the illustration.)

Page 9. Look What I found.
Here are five things I found on the ground when I went for a walk, and three words to describe each thing:

Page 10. The Most

    The loudest thing I can imagine is _____.

    The softest thing I can imagine is _____.

    The funniest thing I can imagine is _____.

    The saddest thing I can imagine is _____.

    The coldest thing I can imagine is _____.

    The hottest thing I can imagine is _____.

    The most surprising thing I can imagine is _____.

    The happiest thing I can imagine is _____.

Once your students are off and running with the pages you suggest to them, they will be quick and eager to devise new ones for themselves and for others in the group. Of course they needn't be restricted to filling in the blanks. They may need or want only a few sample pages before taking off on their own, and members of the group will move at different rates.

When they are ready to organize and write without such structures they will still benefit from brainstorming some representative topics. List the kind of information you and your students feel should be included and let the autobiographical narrative grow accordingly. Here is a list brainstormed by a group of second and third graders and a continuation of it developed by a group of high school students:

    date and place of birth
    names of parents and their ages when you were born
    names and ages of siblings if any
    names of grandparents
    description of the place you lived as a baby
    a baby picture
    a xerox of your birth certificate
    the age at which you first walked and talked
    your first school; how old you were, what you did
    the first birthday you can remember
    any major illnesses you have had
    the funniest thing you can remember

the saddest thing you can remember
the scariest thing you can remember
the happiest thing you can remember
your favorite activities
your fondest wish
   the high school stsudents added:
the places you have lived and for how long
the pets you have owned
the person who has had the greatest influence on your life,
   and why
the person whose life you have influenced and how
the achievement you are proudest of
the three best qualities you see in yourself
three ways in which you hope to grow
a favorite quotation that makes a good punch-line

A fervent believer in the value of autobiography said this to her students. "In the next few weeks we will work on autobiography. This is my year's gift to you. Through it you can catalogue yourself, compare yourself, reveal yourself, and, through thinking about your goals and dreams, direct yourself."

JUNE: JOURNALS

Purpose: Providing daily writing practice

Description: A journal can represent the culmination of all the writer's skills. Weaving together many types of expressive language, the author captures descriptions, events and emotions for his own memories or to share with the outside world. Rich vocabulary, varied constructions, novel connections between categories, combinations of words and pictures, different patterns of organization, prose and poetry all have their places and can be assembled to the author's satisfaction, free from any pre-ordained constraints or rules of right and wrong. Suggestions for journal writers, models and samples follow: a few sprouts of what could be a whole garden of originality, flavor and fulfillment.

Keeping a journal can help an individual focus his attention while sifting and evaluating his experiences and the emotions they generate. Here as in few other places it is safe to be totally honest. A journal provides an accurate view of one's own past. In retrospect our personal landscapes are apt to appear flat, when in truth most of living is hills and valleys. "Oh, last winter? I was depressed the whole time, the weather was lousy, I was tired and had one miserable cold after another. The whole thing was awful!" The speaker's journal, however, tells of a wonderful party, the pride and pleasure when a planter full of paper-white Narcissus bloomed in January, discovering a new author, and the breaking of a log-jam in a friendship which had built up over a misunderstanding. Journals can keep us hopeful in bad times and honest in all times.

A journal can sometimes provide a gift to humanity and posterity. To mention but two classic journal-keepers, surely both literary tradition and countless individuals are richer for *The Diary of Anne Frank* and Anne Morrow Lindbergh's detailed accounts of joy, adventure, tragedy, perplexity and triumph.

A teacher who exposes students to journal-writing, who allows time for it (or who even requires it as part of the curriculum), may start a student on a life-long habit which brings great rewards. And it needn't always be the English teacher who fosters it. A high-school science teacher I know requires each of his students to make a personal, reflective entry in his science notebook at the beginning of every class session. He feels the idea that the arts and sciences should be estranged is outmoded, and he is determined to reinforce the link between the two rather than the separation. At first, the requirement was met with embarrassment, foot shuffling and "I don't know what to put." The teacher, who writes a daily entry himself, read some of his aloud. They varied widely from philosophical musings to irreverent doggerel about national politics, to reactions after seeing a movie or reading a book, and somedays he simply wrote questions. Gradually embarrassment gave way to enthusiasm. Now his students look forward to that five minutes as a time for personal reflection and expression. Oddly, having thought and written, they are at peace intellectually and ready for science. What started as an exercise to enrich science by joining it to the humanities has produced better science students. The same idea could work in a history class, an English class, or a class in a foreign language.

Perhaps journal-writing is a neglected art because it can either seem too amorphous to be worth the bother, or too overwhelming to embrace. The thirteen-year-old girl who receives a fat, square, lockable volume for her birthday titled *My Diary* probably starts out conscientiously to fill the space alotted for each day. Faithful for the first week or so, she soon peters out. Why? Tedium threatens. It is boring to write every evening such entries as, "Today I got up, brushed my teeth, got dressed, and had breakfast. Then I went to school." If it's boring in the beginning there is little incentive to keep going, and if the diary is boring to write it will be deadly for the author to reread.

Since a writer improves his craftsmanship by writing every day, setting up a journal in an appealing format can make sustained practice pleasurable. There are many ways to do this and personal tastes vary so widely that the descriptions offered here are not intended to be dictatorial, but they may help to prime the pump.

First, a suggestion about the volume itself. Books sold commercially as diaries are likely to have small, densely-lined pages about four by five inches, and they provide one page or less for each day. In no way does the physical layout tempt a writer whose handwriting is large or untidy, and it will totally frustrate the writer who crosses out or erases as he goes along.

Instead, the kind of black and white speckled copy book frequently found in schools looks familiar, has nice big pages, and the size of the spaces between the lines is airy and inviting.

Patterns for journal-writing can bring the task to manageable proportions, relieving the writer of the fear that he must record every event of every day. By playing with a variety of patterns for personal recording, we can help a writer select those which match his habits and preferences, which, with luck, will combine to make a rich and rereadable composition.

Patterns for Journals. Explain to your students that straight narrative recording is fine for the student who is a self-starter and has plenty of events and emotions to record. While it is a potentially fruitful approach, it is a difficult one for many students to sustain. Show them how a set of weather symbols can act as a helpful organizer and entry-starter. Ask each student to create a symbol for six different kinds of weather. For example, a boy living in Maine made these:

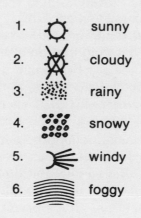

1.   sunny

2.   cloudy

3.   rainy

4.   snowy

5.   windy

6.   foggy

Each day's entry can begin with the appropriate weather symbol. If the journal keeper is full of ideas that day, all well and good. If he isn't sure what to say he can always dip into his bag of descriptive tricks (which he practiced in January) and use them to describe the day's climate and its effect on his mood or activities.

Journal-writing time should never feel like an exam, and some students panic if they think they are running out of ideas. Let the group make a list of *Starters If You're Stuck.* The mere process of thinking them up will help recalcitrant students shed their timidities. Post the list in plain sight. Here is a sample list:

Starters if You're Stuck

1. an adjective that describes today
2. an analogy describing today
3. a couplet describing today
4. a sentence about today using the word *but*
5. a word describing what my family thought of me today
6. the most endearing personal quality I displayed today
7. the least friendly thing I did today
8. the funniest thing that happened today
9. something pleasant I heard on the radio or TV today
10, something I wish today
11. a word sprint for today: as many words as I can write down in one minute which remind me of today
12. something kind to say about my friend
13. five words describing the appearance of my room
14. something I am glad I didn't have to do today
15. three scary things to imagine
16. three qualities I inherited from my mother
17. three qualities I inherited from my father
18. the names of three people in politics, international affairs or sports who were in the evening news and an adjective to describe each one
19. a summary of something I read today
20. an adjective describing my financial condition

Hypothetical Journals. The previous suggestions are for recording the experiences of real people. However, journal and diary writing can be done from other points of view, too. For instance, Sonia Valentine, a third-grade teacher in our school, launches her class into a simulation game in which groups of three or four students must buy or rent ships, sail them across the ocean, land in North America, and survive by hunting, fishing, trading, and building settlements. One member of the group is the diarist who must make a daily record of events and personal reactions to them. According to the rules of the game, each group is given a sum of money (imaginary, of course) at the outset, and each day of the game they must draw three situation cards to determine what happens to them. The situation cards have good news and bad news, require outlays of cash, thwart plans or advance them, and generally describe the kind of happenings early pilgrims and settlers experienced. The diarist must empathize with the emotions of the group and be able to put himself completely in the shoes of one of the participants in order to produce a convincing or interesting saga. This kind of journal writing is drama on paper. The possibilities for such simulation writing are unlimited. Here are some sample entries from our third grade which may help another group get going:

"Our ship is still in port. We must make repairs to the hull before we set out, and we are short of money. All are discouraged."

"Finally our ship is seaworthy. We sold some of our animals to another crew to raise money. We sail at high tide tomorrow. We have checked our provisions and stowed them carefully. Some of the children are afraid, and the pigs make an awful noise, but we are ready."

"A storm at sea has blown us 50 miles off course. The winds are still heavy, the seas are very rough, and many people are seasick."

"It is good to be on land. Even after three weeks we don't take the feeling for granted. Our hunters were successful today and we will have food enough for all."

Although the above are samples from a specific simulation game, I include them because the principle works in many other situations.

Hypothetical journals, which might be called *Other Voices*, can be written from the point of view of a minor character in a story, a person in a different time in history, someone living in a distant part of today's world, or another person in the writer's immediate surroundings. The student who has experienced the feeling of being caught up in a story, who has practiced pretending and has developed a sense of audience will approach this joyfully and skillfully. Here is a sample to offer your students and a list of other possibilities. Add to it.

Read *Snow White*. Pay particular attention to the characters of the dwarfs. Your journal will be based on this sequel to the story: "And in due course, Prince Charming, in gratitude to the dwarfs for their loving attention to his bride, gave each dwarf an entry to the twentieth century and invited him to quaff the Potion of Increase. Thus it was that each little man, now grown to full stature, arrived in an American town or city last month." Write a hypothetical journal chronicling his new life: his occupation, goals, family, difficulties and so forth. Please conclude your journal with this teaser: "There will be no entry in my journal tomorrow, for every year on the anniversary of the breaking of Snow White's spell, seven chairs are mysteriously empty at seven dinner tables, while the old friends gather with a prince and princess in a land not to be found on the maps of today."

Here is a list of other suggestions.

Write a daily journal from the point of view of other characters in *Snow White*. Try telling the story from the point of view of the wicked queen, the king, a dwarf, an animal in the forest.

Write a journal from the point of view of a favorite character in a beloved book. It can cover episodes not part of the plot but from your own imagination, or it can parallel the existing story line. One *Charlotte's Web* enthusiast wrote *The Daily Doubts and Reflections of Templeton the Rat*.

Write the events of your own day, week or month as they would be described by a pessimist such as A.A. Milne's Eeyore, and that treacly optimist Pollyanna. Write the entries in two colors of ink, and have a double entry for each day.

Write your daily, weekly or monthly experiences as they would seem to a person who has just arrived in your type of surroundings. If you live in the city, describe your life from the point of view of a country dweller and vice versa.

Write about your school life, home life and free time activities as if you were a reporter sent to observe a person of unusual interest.

Write a journal from a different period of history: *Struggle for Survival; By Covered Wagon to California; The First Year: Recollections of a Homesteader; Opportunity in the Stars: Observations of the Youngest Person to Spend a Year in Space.*

Write from the point of view of someone in your immediate surroundings. Try a daily entry about family experiences told through the eyes and voice of your mother, father, brother or sister.

Actual Journals. Hypothetical journals can be preliminaries or companions to actual journals. Having launched your students on this endeavor during the school year, plead with them to keep going over the summer and to show you bits and pieces (if they are willing) when school reconvenes in September. Even if you won't be their official teacher, you can always arrange to meet. In looking ahead to what you hope they will accumulate in their journals, encourage them to include vignettes that involve each of the six *wh* words (who, what, when, where, why, how). A description of a person, place, episode, time or explanation will probably be vividly written when it is immediate, and who knows when a powerful description of a vicious dog, a sunrise, or the reason for an argument will be just what the writer needs to complete a story. Being able to retrieve such an element, fresh from personal experience, gives the author permanent access to his own reactions and perceptions. Accumulating pieces of writing in all six *wh* categories gives the writer a rich supply of the elements of all memorable stories, which is to say the elements of living.

A writer's power and imagination are fed by the events and emotions he experiences. Too often we walk briskly through the days of our lives, not stopping to savor, sort, and store our potential treasures. The simple process of choosing patterns and categories for journal-writing can make us more aware of the things that happen around and inside us. Ideas and experiences committed to paper are more likely to stick in our memories because of the effort involved in expressing them. Whether a journal is kept in private, as a preliminary to other writing, or as a publication to be shared with the world, the process itself is invaluable.

Journal-keeping is the hand-clasp of partnership between living and writing.

Index